PRAISE FOR
ONE CHURCH, MANY TRIBES

God has never been as limited as His people in lovingly disseminating and embracing the gospel through diverse native cultures and paradigms. Richard Twiss opens our eyes to the heritage and wonders of our First Nation brothers and sisters and their unique expression of true Christianity.

Ché Ahn
Author of *Into the Fire*
Senior Pastor, Harvest Rock Church
Pasadena, California

Richard Twiss has given us an outstanding, long-needed book that will help bring compassion and reconciliation between diverse peoples created in the image of God and for whom Christ died. Highly recommended.

Bill Bright
Author of *Red Sky in the Morning*
Cofounder, Campus Crusade for Christ
Orlando, Florida

I have often been blessed by the host people of our land, but this book brought a depth of understanding I never possessed. Richard Twiss, whom I have known and admired for years, shows us how Native American culture can reveal new dimensions of the greatness of our Creator. This revolutionary book has the power to change our nation!

Bobbye Byerly
Director of Prayer and Intercession, World Prayer Center
Colorado Springs, Colorado

Richard Twiss has a great heart for reconciliation and for reaching the world with the gospel of Christ. Earnest readers will be enriched and challenged with the profound insights he shares. I pray that God will use this thoughtful book to move many of us to reach out to Native Americans with the compassion and understanding of our Lord, Jesus Christ!

Paul A. Cedar
Chairman, Mission America, Palm Desert, California

The Creator has raised up His servant Richard Twiss for such a time as this. In *One Church, Many Tribes*, Richard captures the problem we face today in ministering to the host people of this land and presents a powerful, well-balanced, culturally relevant means to successfully reach the First Nations people.

Raymond M. Dunton
Hopi/Diné (Navajo)
Founder and Director of WINGS of Freedom,
a ministry of Freedom in Christ
La Habra, California

Richard Twiss carries in his soul God's heart for North America's Native peoples. He is one of those gifted individuals who sees past the illusion of traditions, past deceptions that have kept Christians divided. I pray that God will raise up thousands of disciples who, like Richard, will follow Jesus into the healing of the nations.

Francis Frangipane
Pastor, River of Life Ministries
Cedar Rapids, Iowa

Richard Twiss is a modern-day apostle for the new millennium. The Native American voice is critically needed for the successful completion of the mission work of the Church. As a new generation of believers leaves behind old stereotypes, *One Church, Many Tribes* will be a valuable resource, directly confronting an old worldview that must yield to the overwhelming power of truth.

Rev. Mary A. Glazier
Founder and President, Windwalkers International
Anchorage, Alaska

Jesus is calling every tribe and nation to come together to worship Him in the diversity and beauty of who He made each of us to be.

Melody Green
CEO, Last Days Ministries

I heartily endorse the message of *One Church, Many Tribes*, because I share it fully. Wampum is a beaded belt containing symbols representing an agreement reached between two covenant partners. My wampum belt with Richard Twiss would picture two men joining hands and holding up the cross of Christ.

Rev. Adrian Jacobs
Cayuga from the Six Nations Iroquois Confederacy
Director, Wesleyan Native American Ministries
Rapid City, South Dakota

Richard Twiss has a message that needs to be heard by the Church, Native Americans and the world. It's a message of inclusion and cooperation in which the Church recognizes the contributions of Native American Christians. It's a message of affirmation of Native American culture and compassion for First Nations people. It's a message of the gospel of Jesus Christ preached without compromise to all people.

Stephen B. Kellough
Chaplain of the College, Wheaton College
Wheaton, Illinois

Following the examples of Jesus and the apostle Paul, Richard Twiss seeks to present the gospel relevantly to Native Americans, a neglected people who for too long have been required to abandon their own way of life to become Christians.

Dr. Charles H. Kraft
Professor of Anthropology, School of World Mission
Fuller Theological Seminary
Pasadena, California

After reading *One Church, Many Tribes*, I am convinced of the rightness of the direction of Richard Twiss and his ministry, Wiconi International. In fact, I believe his approach will be absolutely essential if we are to successfully minister to the First Nations of North America. He has my heartfelt and full support.

Rev. Terry LeBlanc
Mi'kmaq Nation, Acadian
Manager, Aboriginal Programs, World Vision Canada

Wesleyan Native American Ministries has seen lives transfomed as a result of these biblical principles. During a seminar where Richard Twiss taught from *One Church, Many Tribes*, the lives of many Native American people were changed forever. We believe the biggest downfall of Christian outreach to Native people is that of condemning the Native culture. Richard's teaching from Scripture that we can be Christians and Native Americans at the same time opened our eyes to lost opportunities and future options for Christ's work.

Larry Marshall
General Director, Wesleyan Native American Ministries
Rapid City, South Dakota

With a perfect blend of intriguing personal stories, vignettes from history, biblical principles and cross-cultural applications, *One Church, Many Tribes* cries out to the Church, inviting Christians everywhere to understand and stand together with First Nations people. One cannot read this book without feeling a profound call to repentance and reconciliation. Richard Twiss pulls at your spiritual heartstrings in a way that doesn't leave you buried in guilt—he motivates you to action!

F. Douglas Pennoyer
Dean of the School of Intercultural Studies, Biola University
La Mirada, California

Richard Twiss presents a much needed and creative approach to ministry in and through the Native American community. What a heart he has for the gospel, for Native Americans and for a biblical approach to accomplishing the work of the Lord!

Tom Phillips
President and CEO, International Students, Inc.

You need to read this book. I first heard of Richard Twiss many years ago, that this Sioux pastor had a heart to reach his First Nations people. Now that I have come to know Richard, I see that this is true; but I also see that he has a heart to bring reconciliation to all people groups within the Body of Christ. Look out world! This warrior is armed with knowledge and is dangerous with the love of Christ!

Grand Chief Lynda Prince
Founder and President, First Nations of North America
Richmond, British Columbia

Richard Twiss, a Lakota/Sioux living in predominantly Anglo America, reminds me of Joseph, long-ago leader of a Hebrew minority in ancient Egypt. To be sure, the Egyptians gave Joseph good cause to feel cynical about Egyptian people. But Joseph, rising above cynicism, blessed an undeserving nation—a nation that had enslaved him and put him in chains without cause. Native Americans have at least as much cause for cynicism about the Anglo population today. Richard Twiss, like a modern Joseph, is calling Christian Native people to rise above cynicism and fulfill a Joseph-like destiny in this strife-ridden world. The message in this marvelous book is like a healing balm for many racial wounds inflicted over time.

Don Richardson
Author of *Peace Child* and *Eternity in Their Hearts*
Woodland Hills, California

Richard Twiss is beating the drum for Native evangelism to be accepted and supported throughout the Church and beyond. He fervently desires that Native Americans be allowed to make their God-given contribution to the world, that Native dancers and singers be invited into our services as full and equal partners in the gospel of Christ. This book is a must for all who would enlist to make war for the kingdom of God in the end times. Until and unless we examine the logs in our own eyes, we will not be able to heal our broken and tattered world. *One Church, Many Tribes* is a major lamp of revelation for the cleansing and healing of America and the world.

John Loren Sanford
Osage Indian
Cofounder, Elijah House, Inc.
Board Member, Native American Resource Network
Hayden, Idaho

Don't read this book unless you are willing to face your own fears, prejudices and possible misperceptions. Richard Twiss has lovingly uncovered my stereotypical thinking and challenged me to a new paradigm concerning his First Nations people. I've long cherished his friendship and now commend him for writing this most important book!

Eddie Smith
President, U.S. Prayer Track
Houston, Texas

Richard Twiss challenges us on some difficult and sensitive issues—issues that have deep roots in this nation and must be addressed. History belongs to the Lord, and this book will give you the desire to seek God's heart in these difficult matters. From God's perspective we will find grace and more understanding that will enable us to love one another in our differences and be participants with Him in fulfilling His desired destiny for the First Nations and for all of America.

Jean Steffenson
President, Native American Resource Network
Castle Rock, Colorado

The folly of attempting to do God's work with man's agenda is never so glaring as in the realm of evangelism. Religious ignorance has wreaked untold damage and misery among indigenous peoples, tribes and races during the last 2,000 years—epecially among the indigenous Native American people.

There are "indigenous" eccentricities among us, whether we live in Detroit or at Wounded Knee, whether we call ourselves Lakota or Latino. The same precious blood was shed on the Cross for us all, and we need every precious drop. Richard Twiss is determined with this book to make Christ's priorities our own priorities in cross-cultural evangelism. *One Church, Many Tribes* is not merely another book about Native Americans. This is a book about God's heart for Jerusalem, Judea, Samaria and the uttermost parts of the earth. I heartily recommend it to you.

Tommy Tenney
The GodChasers.network
Pineville, Louisiana

One Church, Many Tribes is an excellent orientation to a Native American worldview, written in terms the rest of us can understand and appreciate. God is using Richard Twiss in a remarkable way as a leader who is hearing what the Spirit is saying to the churches.

C. Peter Wagner
President, Global Harvest Ministries
Colorado Springs, Colorado

Richard Twiss's vision and commitment to spread the gospel of Jesus Christ through innovative methods that do not condemn the cultures of Native people makes my heart glad. I wholeheartedly endorse and support his vision for Wiconi International and the message of *One Church, Many Tribes*.

Dr. Jerry Yellowhawk
Lakota/Sioux Nation
District Superintendent, Wesleyan Native American Ministries
Rapid City, South Dakota

ONE CHURCH
MANY TRIBES

RICHARD TWISS

Regal
A Division of Gospel Light
Ventura, California, U.S.A.

Published by Regal Books
From Gospel Light
Ventura, California, U.S.A.
Printed in U.S.A.

Regal Books is a ministry of Gospel Light, an evangelical Christian publisher dedicated to serving the local church. We believe God's vision for Gospel Light is to provide church leaders with biblical, user-friendly materials that will help them evangelize, disciple and minister to children, youth and families.

It is our prayer that this Regal book will help you discover biblical truth for your own life and help you meet the needs of others. May God richly bless you.

For a free catalog of resources from Regal Books and Gospel Light, please call your Christian supplier or contact us at 1-800-4-GOSPEL *or* www.regalbooks.com.

Cover Design by Robert Williams
Interior Design by Rosanne Richardson
Edited by Kathi Mills and David Webb

Library of Congress Cataloging-in-Publication Data
Twiss, Richard, 1954–
       One church, many tribes/ Richard Twiss.
             p.   cm.
       Includes bibliographical references.
       ISBN 0-8307-2545-8 (trade paper)
             1. Indians of North America—Religion. 2. Christianity and culture—North America.
       3. Indigenous peoples—Religion. I. Title.

E98.R3 T85   2000
277'.0089'97—dc21   00-025895

       7 8 9 10 11 12 13 14 15 16 17 18 19 20 / 07 06 05 04 03

Rights for publishing this book in other languages are contracted by Gospel Light Worldwide, the international nonprofit ministry of Gospel Light. Gospel Light Worldwide also provides publishing and technical assistance to international publishers dedicated to producing Sunday School and Vacation Bible School curricula and books in the languages of the world. For additional information, visit www.gospellightworldwide.org; write to Gospel Light Worldwide, P.O. Box 3875, Ventura, CA 93006; or send an e-mail to info@gospellightworldwide.org.an e-mail to info@gospellightworldwide.org.

This book is dedicated to my family, to whom I owe a great debt. Like many Native American believers, the journey of self-discovery has not been an easy road for me nor for my family. For 24 years my wife, Katherine, and our four sons, Andrew, Phillip, Ian and Daniel-Emmett, have watched and loved me through seasons of change and major personal transition.

Katherine, thank you for loving and supporting me before we understood that God was, as you say, rearranging the landscape of our lives. Together we are a great team! I love and appreciate you as my life partner and best friend.

And a special thanks to each of my sons, who have supported and grown with me in discovering their roots, heritage and cultural identity. Boys, each one of you continues to make me a very proud and grateful father.

CONTENTS

FOREWORD

It is January 2000. We are at the World Christian Gathering of Indigenous Peoples, being hosted this year by Australian Aborigines at a retreat in the mountains northwest of Sydney. My son's and mine are among the few white faces in the crowd. The sights and sounds are strange to us, yet glorious.

Our hearts are full. We experience wonder and thanksgiving as each people group uses its language and music to praise God. We also experience grief and remorse as they tell their stories, reliving the pain of the colonial imperial expansion that followed after Columbus's voyages.

Surprisingly, very few of these people are bitter or accusatory. In fact, at one of these events I am called to the front by the Samoan delegation because they want to honor white missionaries. I am asked to stand in representation as the Samoans praise the work of the pioneers who first brought the gospel to their islands so long ago.

Richard Twiss is a man of the Lakota/Sioux tribe. I know him well and I respect his integrity. My heart rejoices when I see him this morning, striding to the meeting in full regalia, sur-

rounded by happy Christians from four or five countries, each
one in native garb and carrying unorthodox instruments of worship such as drums and clapsticks.

What should we say when confronted with a movement like this? I
wonder. *What should we think?* This morning, having been asked
to teach, I simply acknowledge the sins of my culture against
indigenous peoples, admitting that much of our historic conduct was in violation of biblical ethics. I then ask for forgiveness
and then sit down. Far be it from me to comment on the com-
plex cultures I see all around me. It is up to indigenous believers
themselves to separate the precious from the worthless in their
cultures. They know the Bible well and they know their cultures
well.

I've been a missionary for nearly 30 years, and I believe that
what I am seeing this day is an answer to prayer. The worldwide
move of God among indigenous peoples is reminiscent of the
1970s when the symbols of a strange culture, a counterculture,
became central to revival and harvest in the Church. I'm thinking of the Jesus Movement, in which the Fender guitar and electric soft-rock praise became synonymous with the salvation of
millions of the world's youth. Those who prayed for this harvest
almost aborted it through their own harsh criticism, as they
failed to recognize God at work in the alien language, dress and
music of the new generation. We cannot make this same mistake
again.

For many years I have labored alongside those seeking reconciliation and justice for Native Americans. We have often
faced terrible discouragement. Today, however, I see answers to
prayer breaking through like a new dawn.

Most people know me as a North American Christian leader
through my book and public ministry with movements such as
Youth With a Mission and Promise Keepers; but in fact I was

born and raised in New Zealand. I have been deeply involved with the progress of the Church in that nation, and I can testify that what is taught in this book has dramatically proven true in New Zealand: God works from the foundations up. The restoration of the godly inheritance of Maori Christians in New Zealand has become the catalyst for a season of nationwide cleansing and healing in preparation for revival. On that basis I plead with Canadian and American Christians, particularly the intercessors, to turn their hearts toward Native American Christians as they struggle with issues of cultural identity.

In this book, Richard Twiss clearly shows there is a huge difference between cultural relativism and moral relativism. It's not the form that's important; it's the meaning attached to it. I have worked with Richard for many years, closely questioning the First Nations leaders with whom he works about their unique styles of worship. I rarely find evidence of syncretism. Rather, I see a steady insistence on the moral absolutes that flow from biblical revelation of the nature, character and personality of our Creator.

This is an important book for all believers because the struggle to define identity affects us all. However, this is an *essential* book for the First Nations of North America and for indigenous peoples around the world. Well written, easy to read, humorous and full of God's wisdom, this teaching will help you to lead your community to Christ and to give your children the gift of identity.

John Dawson
Founder, International Reconciliation Coalition
Author of *Healing America's Wounds*

ACKNOWLEDGMENTS

I am deeply grateful and indebted to so many who have walked with me through the long process of bringing this manuscript to its published form:

To my friend Rev. John Knight, for his extensive research about Chief Spokane Garry and for his encouragement that I tell Chief Garry's story.

To John Sandford, for praying for me and with me through times of trial and spiritual growth. John, your many hours of editing this manuscript in its early stages were of immeasurable help, as was your mentoring of me as a young writer.

Thank you, John Dawson, for your unfailing encouragement and friendship through some tough times of wondering if all the misunderstanding was worth it.

Thanks to all the folks at New Discovery Community Church who loved me as their senior pastor and endured my 13 years of personal transformation, stages of growth, mistakes and failures.

A very special thank-you to our many friends and supporters who have hung in there with us over the years, when we were trying to hear from the Lord and find our way.

To my Native buds. Lloyd Commander, you were an encouraging sounding board and ally at the beginning of this journey. Adrian Jacobs, Terry LeBlanc, Mary Glazier, Jon Lansa, Garland and Susan Brunoe—each of your friendships is a valuable resource and treasure in my life.

To my Lakota elders, Marrles Moore and Jerry Yellowhawk. Thanks for encouraging me to keep moving ahead.

To those pastors who early on believed in my ministry and supported us—Fred Gulker, Mark Campbell, Glen Johnson, Bob Yarborough, David Knight and Neal Curtiss.

Jean Steffenson, you opened many doors of opportunity for me, for which I am grateful.

To all my Native brothers and sisters. I pray your journey will lead to greater freedom, spiritual wholeness and future generations of spiritually alive and culturally strong children through Jesus Christ, the Creator and Waymaker.

A SLEEPING GIANT

Wind and rain blowing in my face, I carefully took aim and let 'er go. I endured my friends' jeering as it sailed past the Slow Down sign I was aiming at. The empty beer bottle I had just tossed out the rear window of the speeding '66 Chevy Impala SS had whistled off into the dark, rainy night. I was drinking beer and smoking marijuana with a carload of friends, cruising the countryside and having a good time.

My arm was still outside the window when our car suddenly went airborne, and my stomach catapulted into my throat as we became momentarily suspended in midair. The driver of the car had accelerated as we approached a severe drop in the road down a steep hill. All at once, glass was flying everywhere, and I heard a horrible, grinding metal sound. I was stunned and in shock, but I knew that I had been badly injured.

EVERY PART IS VITALLY CONNECTED

I was 17 years old. My arm had been severely mangled in the auto accident. The arm was crushed, the bone broken, muscle torn away and one nerve severed when the driver of the car lost control and we collided with a tractor parked by the road. Initially, the surgeons told me they would have to amputate; but they managed to repair my arm and I slowly healed.

A year later, an infection that had been incubating in the bone of my arm began to surface. At that time we were living in Maui, and a doctor there diagnosed my feeble condition as suffering from a low-grade fever—sickness just below the surface.

Months after seeing the doctor in Hawaii and having moved to Anchorage, Alaska, I became gravely ill and was told by another doctor that, had I delayed coming in to see him for even a few more days, I could easily have died. This was nearly two years after the initial injury, and the infection had spread from my arm to the rest of my body, requiring a month-long hospital stay and four daily injections of intravenous antibiotics.

First Corinthians 12:26 (*NIV*) tells us, "If one part suffers, every part suffers with it." Just as my arm is integrally connected to the rest of my body, so the members of the Church around the world are connected with one another in Jesus Christ. It is my conviction that because of Christian Native Americans' history of suffering and their absence from the evangelical mainstream, the Body of Christ in America suffers from a spiritual low-grade fever.

I have studied the history of missions among the First Nations people—a term denoting original habitation by sovereign people or nations—and I have examined their role in the life of the North American church. It is clear that in the Church, as in the secular culture, a huge disparity exists between the indigenous and immigrant peoples in the land.

No matter how unaware we may be of the reality of our connectedness in Christ, we affect one another, for good or evil. Whatever our inclinations, outside of gross heresy, there is no biblical basis that would allow us to disengage from one another or disregard our need for one another. Paul describes our connectedness in this way: "If the foot should say, 'Because I am not a hand, I do not belong to the body,' it would not for that reason cease to be part of the body" (1 Cor. 12:15, *NIV*).

Unless *all* the various parts that God designed to make up the whole are intact and functioning, there is dysfunction. Each and every part must be connected and engaged, or there is no possible way for the whole to function fully and according to God's design and best plan. Without our Native brethren, the Church only makes do—we limp along, less than we are meant to be.

UNPARALLELED MISSION OPPORTUNITY

When it comes to modern missions, I believe no other people group is so uniquely positioned for world evangelization today as are First Nations people. In part, I've written this book to make the Church aware of this remarkable opportunity for world missions. Heightened awareness of our need for one another as equal partners in the work and mission of the Church will truly honor God and set people free the world over.

Imagine with me this scenario. Picture Native believers, full of passion for God, strength and beauty, using their traditional dance, music and colorful dress to speak to captivated audiences worldwide. Imagine First Nations ministry teams sharing with audiences in public schools, on university campuses and in concert halls across America. I have witnessed and experienced this enough times to know that walls of distrust and suspicion about Christianity melt away. People by the thousands enjoy the cultural celebrations of Native people each year around the world. In recent years there has been a massive surge of interest in

Native American spirituality, New Age tribalism, world music and indigenous arts and dance. Now is the time to take advantage of this interest in First Nations people and their culture to share the freedom and new life possible through Jesus Christ!

At this time in history, almighty God has raised up the First Nations people of North America as a new wave of ambassadors for the gospel of Jesus Christ. I believe it will be teams of indigenous people who will break through into the Islamic nations of the world, bridging our cultures to share the good news. To meet this challenge, I have been assembling cultural teams of Native believers who excel in their traditional-style dances, drum music and personal witness for Jesus Christ. Along with other Native leaders, I have developed seminars and teaching materials to equip believers with a biblical worldview of culture and the Kingdom.

As we near 500 years of missions among the tribes of North America, it is critically important that the Church stop viewing Native people solely as a mission field. Admittedly, there exist great challenges and needs among our people; but our challenges and needs are not the sum total of our identity. This is a *kairos* (appointed) time for First Nations people in the Body of Christ. God is calling the Church to step forward into the new millennium and welcome First Nations believers as valued and needed partners in the Body.

CHANGE IS ALWAYS UNCOMFORTABLE

Jerry Yellowhawk, my *ate* (a term of respect for "father"), told me that he has been waiting his whole life as a Christian—nearly 50 years—to see these cultural changes come to the Church and Native work. This is a time of transition in ministry among indigenous believers around the world—a time of exploration and sincere inquiring of the Lord for new perspectives and approaches to Native ministry. Around the globe among indigenous Christians, cultural identity is surfacing as the key dynamic in this emerging new Native ministry paradigm and spiritual awakening.

This transition is somewhat akin to what happened when the Jesus Movement swept the nation and world in the late 1960s and early '70s. Initially, when the hippies started getting saved, and especially when they started bringing their rock-and-roll-style (read: worldly) music into church on Sunday mornings, many established Christians did not recognize, nor could they embrace, what God was doing. Many rejected this movement because it did not look, act or sound Christian—that is, neither the movement nor its participants behaved according to the established definitions of religious correctness.

The Native church now finds itself in a similar situation. Only now, instead of controversy over the electric guitars and drums now commonplace in our churches, Christians are debating the use of Native American drums, gourds, rattles and dances as legitimate expressions of godly faith. In the next decade or so, this controversy will also subside and we will hear and see indigenous sounds and movements in church services across the land in glorious worship to Jesus Christ. Indeed, that day is already dawning.

"INDIANS" IN A POLITICALLY CORRECT AGE

Since I am a Lakota/Sioux, I am often asked, "What do you prefer to be called? Native American? American Indian?" The various tribes do not agree on an all-encompassing name, but "Native American" would be the most commonly accepted term.

In Canada it has been "Aboriginal" or "First Nations." Others use the terms "host people" or "host nations."

You probably know the story. When Columbus set out to discover a new trade route to the West Indies, he in fact landed in the Caribbean. Thinking he had reached the West Indies, he mistakenly called the first folks he saw Indians. It is often jokingly said by Native people that it's a good thing Columbus didn't think he had found Turkey or we would be called Turkeys today.

I strongly embrace the concept contained in the name "First Nations." The terms "American Indian" and "Native American" both denote a political and colonial identity, created by others and imposed on us through conquest and treaty. That is not our identity.

In my opinion, "First Nations" captures the essence of our biblical identity as a people created in the image of God and not in the image of European culture. The name speaks of independence, sovereignty and self-determination, identifying us as equals in terms of worth and value, not as dependents who find their identity in the approval or patronage of others.

Also, throughout the book I will often use the phrase "indigenous people" in referring to tribal peoples. By this I mean the original inhabitants of a geographic area prior to European colonization.

Though I will be addressing issues as they relate specifically to First Nations and Anglo peoples, it goes without saying that these same issues apply to all peoples and their unique human distinctivenesses. The historical treatment of and current situations among African, Asian, Hebrew and Hispanic Americans are similar in many respects.

The ongoing tensions between male and female, Republican and Democrat, white-collar and blue-collar, conservative and liberal and rich and poor are situations I believe only Christ can adequately mend. What we learn as we struggle to heal the rifts between Natives and Anglos can serve to equip us for accomplishing every other kind of needed reconciliation.

WE ARE IN THIS TOGETHER

Throughout this book, I will introduce you to some basic historical and worldview differences between Euro-American and North American Native peoples. Hopefully, this will give you some valid cultural insights to better appreciate and understand the thinking of modern Native people. I believe this is important because we are all in this together; we all have a part to play in the healing of our nation.

My views and beliefs do not reflect those of all Native leaders. Mine are simply the observations and considerations of a Christian Native American man hoping to see and understand more than he does now. The portrayals of Native culture herein are generalizations. The cultures and socioeconomic conditions among First Nations people vary tremendously from tribe to tribe and from region to region. Many new social dynamics affect our people today. For example, more than half of today's two million Native Americans live in cities, greatly impacting Native cultural stability and identity.

A BETTER TOMORROW

It is my hope that this book will open the eyes of God's people across America—and all other lands—providing them with insights and cultural footholds and teaching them to value and embrace those who are different, especially First Nations people. I have no desire to produce guilt, blame or condemnation in others.

My prayer is that awakened awareness will lead to healing, reconciliation and wholeness for the entire Body of Christ. If we are to accomplish all of God's purposes in these final days of harvest, we must recognize and embrace all the different parts of His Body as necessary and valuable.

The evangelist Billy Graham once said, "The greatest moments of Native history may lie ahead of us if a great spiritual renewal and awakening should take place. The Native American has been a sleeping giant. He is awakening. The original Americans could become the evangelists who will help win America for Christ! Remember these forgotten people!"[1]

Richard Twiss, *Taoyate Obnajin*
("He Stands With His People")
Sicangu Band, Rosebud Lakota/Sioux Tribe
President, Wiconi International

CHAPTER ONE

500 YEARS OF
BAD HAIRCUTS

Wow! I thought, *We are actually here—Jerusalem, the city of the Great King.* As we brushed against people in the narrow, crowded stone streets in the Palestinian sector of the ancient city of Jerusalem, the exotic personality of the city of God was making a deep impression on us. We were absorbed in its sights, smells and sounds when we were startled by a voice yelling at us. We turned to see a Palestinian shop owner shouting from inside his small storefront, "Come, come! You are Red Indians from America, yes?" My friend Garland and I stepped into his small shop and replied that yes, we were Native Americans. The shopkeeper then said with great emotion, "They stole your land! God gave you that land, and you need to fight and take it back!"

As Garland and I talked with the shop owner, we were surprised at the knowledge of and interest in First Nations people shown by this Palestinian who lived on the other side of the world from North America. In the United States, Canada and around the globe, I have found there is a widespread fascination and desire to learn all there is to know about the cultures of First Nations people. In Germany there are numerous Indian clubs scattered across the country. In Great Britain, Buffalo Bill Cody left a legacy of Native American lore that is now more popular than ever. Many in Mongolia believe that Native Americans are their long-lost relatives. In Fiji and New Zealand little boys grow up playing cowboys and Indians—and most want to be the Indians.

This phenomenon, fueled by popular books and theatrical and TV movies like *Dances with Wolves*, *Geronimo* and *Pocahontas*, has created what I believe is an unparalleled open door for the First Nations people to take the gospel of Jesus Christ into the most difficult regions of the world, including America. And yet for five long centuries, Natives have struggled just to find a place of acceptance and recognition of their cultural identity in the Church.

THE WAYS OF OUR PEOPLE HAVE BEEN REJECTED

The historical record of missions among the tribes of North America is a saga marked by enormous potential, great failures and profound sadness. With a few notable exceptions—men like Sir William Johnson, Chief Joseph Brant and Rev. Charles Chauncy—those engaged in eighteenth-century mission work disdained Native American culture and barred it from the churches. Early missionaries failed to recognize and embrace the intrinsic God-given value of the people to whom they were sent—a blindness that has prevailed in the American church to this day.[1]

Dr. Paul Hiebert describes as the "White man's burden" their perceived need to educate and civilize the world. Hiebert explains that the early missionaries to First Nations people brought with them the prevailing European attitudes of the day toward Native North Americans. The missionaries equated Christianity with Western culture and its apparent superiority over other cultural forms and expressions—a supposition not necessarily based on truth but on the "progress" of industry, science and commerce. Clearly, they believed, the West was civilized and the rest of the world primitive:

> The seventeenth-century New England Puritan missionaries largely set the course for modern missions. They defined their task as preaching the gospel so that Native Americans would be converted and receive personal salvation. But early in their missionary experience these New Englanders concluded that Indian converts could only be Christians if they were "civilized." The model by which they measured their converts was English Puritan civilization. The missionaries felt compassion and responsibility for their converts. They gathered these new Christians into churches for nurture and discipline and set up programs to transform Christian Indians into English Puritans.[2]

One effect of this history of bigotry and cultural conquest has been that, to this day, Native North Americans have never experienced the rise of an indigenous church movement or widespread revival. But hope remains that all has not been in vain.

In the providence of almighty God, I believe it was His plan that the White man from across the great water would deliver the sacred message of Jesus to the First Nations of this continent. Our gracious heavenly Father redeems our worst blunders and causes all things to work together for good. Had the roles been reversed, I doubt we Native people would have performed any better than the Europeans.

"Out of sight, out of mind" best describes the Native American situation among American Evangelicals today. You might think that, in this age of tolerance, the Indian and the Eskimo would be free to express themselves as Native Americans in the Church and in society. Yet Native expressions of Christ and His kingdom are all but absent from the mainstream of the White church in America—this despite nearly five centuries of unabated missionary activity!

From the inception of government-sponsored and church-run schools in this land, missionaries made a practice of prepping young Native boys and girls by cutting their hair in a uniform style, a custom that continued until the early 1900s. As much as anything, these haircuts symbolized an attempt to civilize Native American young people and turn them into good little Englishmen, Dutchmen, Frenchmen, etc. Bad haircuts were but one example of forced changes and the replacement of traditional clothing, language and culture—changes that were a denial of a people's God-given identity and existence. If I can be so bold, this approach to missions could legitimately be viewed as a kind of cultural genocide.

Metaphorically, after 500 years it's time for the Body of Christ to let First Nations people choose their own hairstyles. Given so few believers among the 3.5 million Native North Americans, many are asking, Why not try some new ways of doing church among Native people?

In the past few years, I have grown my hair long, and now I often wear it in braids. Hudson Taylor, a great missionary to China and one of my heroes in the faith, also grew his hair long and wore it in a braid, while adopting the clothing styles of the people to whom he ministered. Consequently, he was seen by his British comrades as rejecting their ways and therefore was kicked out of the missionary compound. Taylor went on to become one of the Kingdom's most fruitful missionaries ever.

I am using haircuts as an analogy to describe the Church's historical rejectionist approach to missions among tribal peoples around the world. By and large, Native American people have not found the new life and freedom promised in the gospel of Jesus Christ but, rather, have experienced ongoing pain within a Western culture that is both alien and condemning, even genocidal against indigenous people.

However, a new day is upon us, as indigenous people of this land are revitalizing their languages, restoring familial kinship systems and rediscovering their music, dances and art forms in Jesus Christ—all for the glory of God!

IT IS A GOOD DAY TO DIE!

As the drums pounded and war songs were sung that night, we danced and prepared ourselves to fight for our lives. All around us the building was becoming filled with hysteria, rage and confusion. Leonard Crow Dog, a Lakota/Sioux medicine man from the Rosebud Reservation, offered prayers of purification and blessing as he painted the faces of many of the men and women who were armed and ready for war. We shouted the words of the great Sioux chief Crazy Horse, "Hoka Hey!" meaning "It is a good day to die!" This cry of the 600 men, women and children—all warriors—assembled that day meant that this would be a good a day to die in battle with honor. My heart, which was already pounding, thumped with increasing intensity as we prepared ourselves for the imminent charge of the federal marshals and their dogs, tear gas and weaponry.

On that late November afternoon in 1972, I stood four stories up on the roof of the Bureau of Indian Affairs (BIA) office building in Washington, DC. We had forced all the BIA employees to leave; then we had chained the doors and taken control of the building. In the early evening several federal marshals were allowed in and they gave us an ultimatum: "Vacate the building in one hour or be removed by force." We did not move. This well-worn stone building represented to us the centuries of governmental injustice, oppression and impoverishment Native people had experienced in America. Now, looking out from the roof I could see many famous Washington landmarks, while below me 300 police arrived in full riot gear and surrounded us.

I was part of the American Indian Movement's (AIM) Trail of Broken Treaties protest. We were expressing Indian peoples' frustration and anger over the U.S. government's unjust breaking of nearly all the hundreds of treaties they had made with the First Nations tribes. Ours was a cry from the First Nations for justice.

The government threats to remove us forcefully from the building only made us angrier. Official documents and papers were strewn over almost every square inch of all four stories. We reinforced the windows with duct tape and distributed water barrels with towels in anticipation of tear gas. We fashioned weapons of all kinds: spiked clubs, bows and arrows, deadly spears, gas bombs and a small arsenal of guns—articles of war. I later learned that a number of women had smuggled into the building a large amount of dynamite taped to their bodies. At one point several of us were given a dozen gas-filled light bulbs and were instructed to set the building on fire, beginning on the top floor and working our way to the bottom. Fortunately, the idea was quickly scrapped.

After eight extremely intense days of threats, ultimatums and moments of hysteria, I couldn't have been more relieved when our siege came to a peaceful end. Fortunately, the marshals never did storm the building. Neverthless, we had exploded with long pent-up bitterness, anger and frustration. One afternoon during the siege, I found myself jumping out of the way to avoid a Native man who was swinging a pipe, indiscriminately shattering every object he could, his violent outburst like the fuse on a keg of dynamite. Native Americans had stored up generations of anger and frustration, and some of us were prepared to take whatever actions might seem necessary to bring about change in Indian America. Our detonation resulted in more than two million dollars worth of damage! We had ransacked the entire office building, stripping it of every item of value.

At the time, we felt confident that we had made our point. Though, subsequently, little changed politically, the Native American voice had exploded into the public eye.

THE JESUS WAY

Back in my aunt's home on the Rosebud Sioux Reservation in South Dakota, the thrill of DC soon wore off. I found myself both disillusioned and disappointed with AIM. I saw the same hypocrisy among the leaders of AIM that I had seen in the lives of other political and spiritual leaders. One night I watched one of the movement's most respected spiritual leaders come staggering out of a local reservation bar with a woman under each arm. As a result, I began drifting deeper into drug and alcohol abuse. And because AIM was initially born out of the experience of urban Native leaders, at times it created strife and violent clashes among tribal members on many reservations.

I left the reservation and traveled back to the Pacific Northwest, where I hooked up with my old drinking buddies in Oregon. Before long, though, I wanted to escape into the mountains and connect spiritually with a sense of identity and purpose for my life. So I left my mom's house in Silverton, Oregon, and moved north to the state of Washington to plant trees. In November 1973, while living out of my hippie/Indian van, I had a brush with the law in a small lumber town, resulting in a few days in jail for alcohol abuse and possession of marijuana. Because my blood-alcohol content was so high at the time of my arrest, the judge concluded that I must have had a severe drinking problem and sent me to a drug rehabilitation program as a condition of my release. Instead of complying with his order, I talked a friend into moving with me to Maui.

There I was drawn to the Eastern religions: Buddhism, Taoism, Hinduism. Still searching for meaning in my life, I practiced yoga, prayed mantric prayers and sought enlightenment through the use of hallucinogenic drugs. I spent many nights praying and sleeping under the stars. But the combination of drugs, Eastern religions, my Catholic upbringing and Native American spirituality only led to further confusion. When I wasn't searching for God, I partied with friends and tried relationships with a number of women. I felt empty inside. I knew there had to be more to life than what I was experiencing.

While hitchhiking to the other side of Maui one afternoon, I was picked up by a couple of guys who talked to me about God, about Jesus Christ and His plan for my life. I thought they were narrow-minded, self-righteous Jesus freaks and Bible thumpers, and after giving them a piece of my mind, I got out of the car. Of course, I had read about and understood the destructive impact Christianity had worked among many of our Indian tribes historically, and I saw it as nothing but the destructive religion of the White man. The last thing I wanted was to be a Christian. But then a few weeks later, while alone on a beach in Maui, I remembered what these two Christian men had said to me about Jesus.

There is a place on the coast of Maui called the Seven Sacred Pools, where a small river cascades down a valley in a series of waterfalls. In a nearby meadow, physlicibin mushroom plants—a very strong hallucinogenic—grew in great numbers. Often, many spiritual seekers could be found there picking and eating the plants and tripping out. One day, I had eaten numerous magic mushrooms (as they are referred to in street jargon) and at 2:30 in the morning, I found myself completely engulfed in paranoia and the fear of dying or losing my mind. I tried my Eastern meditations and prayers for relief, but to no avail. I could imagine going crazy and running down the beach with men in white uniforms chasing me. It was a horrible moment mentally and emotionally.

At last, fearing the worst, I literally yelled at the top of my lungs, "Jesus, if You're real and You can do what those people said You could do, then I want You to come into my heart and life and to forgive me for the wrong I've done!" At that moment an incredible thing happened. The effect of the drugs left, the fear disappeared, and the most incredible sensation of peace flooded my being from the top of my head to the bottom of my feet. I felt clean, forgiven and filled with joy.

It was there on that beach that the Creator revealed Himself to me in the person of Jesus Christ, and I became a follower of the Jesus Way.

"JUST BE LIKE US"

Several months after committing my life to Jesus Christ in Maui, I traveled to Alaska to visit a friend from school who was involved with a Christian training center called the Bread of Life Bakery. My friend was part of Gospel Outreach (GO), a Christian ministry dedicated to evangelism and to training for ministry. Founded by an apostolic leader named Jim Durkin, GO was one of many ministries birthed out of the Jesus Movement of the 1970s. With the exception of one African-American and a few Alaska natives who came and went, GO was primarily an Anglo ministry.

A growing number of

Native American believers

use the term "the Jesus Way"

to describe their faith.

I remember that a few months after I had begun living at the training center in the beautiful Matanuska Valley north of Anchorage, I began to wonder how my Lakota heritage could be part of my new Christian experience—especially after recently going through the AIM experience.

So one afternoon I asked one of the pastoral leaders how I was supposed to relate to my Native culture as a Christian. I distinctly remember him opening the Bible he was carrying and reading from Galatians 3:28 (*NIV*), where Paul wrote, "There is neither Jew nor Greek, slave nor free, male nor female, for you are all one in Christ Jesus." After reading the passage, this pastoral leader commented on how cultures should all blend together for us as Christians. He then concluded, "So, Richard, don't worry about being Indian; *just be like us.*"

Though he was perhaps unaware of it, essentially what he was saying was, "Forget your Indianness and embrace our White culture as the *only* Christian culture." Being young and naive and sincerely committed to becoming a wholehearted follower of Jesus, I listened. After all, I was a baby in the faith and a more knowledgeable leader had given me what seemed to be a reasonable Christian perspective about cultures. So for the next eight years I lived the Christian life as it was culturally modeled for me by non-Native friends and Christian brethren. I have since found this way of life to be less than who I am—and much less than the Lord wants me to be!

A growing number of evangelical Native believers are using the term "the Jesus Way" to describe their faith in Jesus Christ. This phrase speaks of a way of life, a trail we walk on and live by. Some Lakota people speak of Jesus as *Chanku*, "the Road" or "the Way." Jesus said of Himself, "I am the way, the truth, and the life" (John 14:6).

The Jesus Way presents Jesus Christ to the nonbelieving Native in terms that are more in line with the way Native people approach life. Among nonbelieving Indians the word "Christianity" has come to mean only the abusive religion of the White man.

Often when I speak of faith in Jesus Christ, I refer to myself and others as followers of the Jesus Way.

LIFE ON THE RESERVATION

I was born on the Rosebud Reservation among my mother's people. Life was a blast growing up in Rosebud, a town of 600 where everyone was acquainted. I have many fond memories of the reservation. My six- and seven-year-old buddies and I walked around town, visited the local store, got into trouble, went swimming at the reservoir, explored the dump, stayed out late in the summers—a kid's paradise.

I especially loved the powwows. The powwow was a time for observing and participating in the cultural activities of the tribe, a time for strengthening family relationships. The colors and beauty of the traditional regalia were awesome to behold, and I admired the athleticism and grace of the dancers. The booming rhythm of the drums inspired my young Native heart. These gatherings left an indelible impression of the value and beauty of being Native American.

But there was another, darker side of reservation life: alcoholism and violence. My mother did not want us to grow up in that atmosphere, and she wanted us to learn to be successful in the White man's world. So we moved from the reservation, first to Denver, then to Klamath Falls, Oregon, and eventually to Silverton, near Salem, where I attended school from the 3rd through 12th grades. During those years we made several summer visits to Rosebud to visit with our relatives.

My mom is an amazing woman. As a single mother, she worked full-time as a nurse at night, refusing to accept the aid of welfare and food stamps though she was raising four kids. My mom is a strong, nonverbal woman, beautiful and dignified. No matter how much trouble I got into, she always loved and accepted me. This is not to say she didn't get after me when I was being a rebellious teenager. In fact, she locked me out of the house a time or two while she went to work at night.

Unfortunately, my mom married an abusive alcoholic from back home on the rez (reservation). He used to beat my mom, and I spent many frightening nights crying with my half brother and sisters and listening to my mom and her husband fight. I can remember dreaming about the day when I would be big enough to beat him up. They divorced when I was 9 or 10, and my mom never remarried.

After graduating from high school, I moved back to the Rosebud Reservation to attend Sinte Gleska College, where I became involved in AIM. It was during this time that I began to reconnect with my relatives and their culture.

SOME HISTORY OF FIRST NATIONS PEOPLE

It is said that those who win the wars get to write the history books. Most recorded history is actually a very subjective accounting of past events. People with pen and paper sit down and attempt to accurately and ethically describe *their* perceptions of events they have seen, heard about and researched—a far cry from any guarantee of accuracy.

Let's imagine for a moment that First Nations people had won the war for the North American continent. Our historian, Sees Far, writes that on a warm, windless morning, Caribbean tribes discovered and rescued a strange chief and his crew. The tribes had never seen such a canoe or men who looked like these. Intrigued by what and whom they had discovered on their shore, the tribes showed customary protocol and cared for their uninvited guests. They fed and nursed the men back to health. They helped supply them with food, fresh water and other goods and then wished them well in their journey back to their country far away.

U.S. history tells the story this way: Christopher Columbus was a brave and courageous visionary who discovered a new world that would later become America. Until Columbus's arrival, the native people of this new land were "undiscovered."

Sees Far might have recorded a First Nations perspective of this event as the arrival of a lost chief of a tribe who turned out not to be new friends but marauding invaders. His record of history might have witnessed these guests returning after many moons with many more canoes filled with enemy warriors, greedily lusting after the First Nations people's gold metal and bringing great destruction and death to the First Nations' way of life.

So which of the two historical perspectives is the most accurate? In today's political stewpot of conservative politics, Sees Far may be accused of presenting a revisionist, non-Christian spin on U.S. history. Yet as a fellow believer in Christ, please allow me to challenge your assumptions about nationalism, patriotism and Christian love. Which do you believe is the more accurate record and why? I think both are equally inaccurate and accurate—it is a neither-and-both dynamic.

We Cannot Walk the Path of Our Ancestors

Five hundred years after the arrival of the White man, Native people and their cultures have managed to survive despite the Europeans' misguided attempts at evangelization and oppression. America has often been referred to as the melting pot of the world. A Native man once said about Native people and their place in this supposed culturally homogenized melting pot, "Whatever it is that Indian people are made out of, we don't melt too easy."

The First Nations have often been viewed as obstacles to the civilization, development and cultivation of this land. L. Frank Baum, author of the classic children's story *The Wizard of Oz*, wrote in the *Aberdeen Saturday Pioneer* in 1890:

> With his fall the nobility of the Redskin is extinguished, and what few are left are a pack of whining curs who lick the hand that smites them. The whites, by law of conquest and by justice of civilization, are master of the

American continent, and the best safety of the frontier settlements will be secured by the total annihilation of the few remaining Indians.[3]

The "total annihilation" of Native people was once considered a legitimate approach to solving the Native problem. And it almost happened.

Estimates of the pre-Columbus Indian population range from 1 million to 30 million, depending upon the criteria used. Many historians use a conservative figure of 10 to 12 million. If this is true, then the following facts are most disturbing:

- By 1900 only 237,000 Native people were left in the United States.
- In the early 1800s, California was home to an estimated 260,000 Indians. By 1900, there were 20,000.
- Today nearly 2 million self-declared Native Americans live in the United States. Another 1.3 million live in Canada.
- According to the 1990 census, 23 percent of the Native population live on reservations; 77 percent live in urban areas.
- There are 557 federally recognized tribes, or nations; 220 of those are in Alaska. Another 150 tribes are in the process of petitioning for federal recognition.
- Approximately 200 Native tribes have become extinct.
- There are 250 different Native languages and dialects still spoken on a daily basis. (Apache and Lakota are as different from Navajo and Mohawk as Norwegian is from Japanese.)

- Fewer than 10 percent of contemporary Indians speak their Native languages.
- The federal government recognizes 300 reservations, which take up less than 4 percent of the land in the continental United States.
- About 11 million acres of land within reservation boundaries (20 percent) are owned by non-Indians.
- Nearly one-half of reservation populations are non-Indian.[4]

George Russell writes that "furthermore, each tribe claims rights as a sovereign nation, each with its own agenda and concerns. The legal ramifications are a quagmire of overlapping state and federal judicial systems." He goes on to say:

> Indians are a durable and resourceful people. They have survived 400 years of genocide and 100 years of Bureau of Indian Affairs dominance and government control. For the moment the pendulum of social conscience has swung in favor of Indians. Empathy is wonderful, however Indians must control their own destiny. The idea that Native people can live in tranquil harmony with nature on reservations is an illusion. Today's Indians cannot walk the path their ancestors walked.[5]

Pilgrims, Colonists and Early Beginnings
During President Bill Clinton's second term in office, the United States experienced a minor immigration crisis as a small flood of "boat people" made their way from Cuba and Haiti hoping to gain illegal entry into Florida. When I was a teenager, then-President Lyndon Johnson experienced a similar crisis with immigrants

streaming in from Cambodia, Vietnam and Thailand.

From a First Nations perspective the crisis began when that first boatload of immigrants hit Plymouth Rock!

Bemoaning the injustices Indian people have faced at the hands of European immigrants, a Native once said, "We should have had stricter immigration laws." Someone else said, "We gave them an inch and they took 6,000 miles!"

Every fourth Thursday in November, Americans celebrate the Pilgrims' survival of their first winter on the shores of this land. In schools across the land, children perform Thanksgiving plays recounting the story of how Indians taught the Pilgrims to plant corn and to hunt deer and turkeys. One year at this time I spoke to a group of fourth graders, and during my usual question-and-answer session, a little boy asked me, "Are you a real Indian or are you a person?"

Even if Americans have idealized and romanticized the Pilgrims and their struggles in a strange new land, that first flush of goodwill between the settlers and Native Americans was short-lived. History paints a much more sordid and brutal reality for the First Nations people and their relationships with those who came a few short years later on the heels of the Pilgrims.

It is well known that there were two basic streams of immigrants to America: One came for essentially religious reasons, the other for financial gain. One group represented the best of people who, for the most part, came as ambassadors of Jesus Christ, while the other came seeking wealth, riches and fame.

From the very beginning, misunderstanding, lack of respect and eventually hatred toward Native Americans were evident among the immigrants; and these attitudes were passed down to each progressive generation of European settlers in the colonies. When Native Americans welcomed and helped the White man, the Natives were viewed as simple pagans who obviously did not deserve this great land, as adolescents who could be easily manipulated and cheated at will. For every positive portrayal of tribal life in the 1600s and 1700s, countless negative portrayals were penned by European explorers, traders and settlers. Until recently the negative accounts were so commonly accepted that scholars have a difficult time today separating fact from fiction.

After visiting New York and meeting with some local Native people, I learned, for example, how the European directors of the Dutch West Indies Company had carefully planned their New Amsterdam colony on Manhattan Island. Like most early immigrants they came with the best of intentions and, I believe, planned to build good relationships with the Native Americans and develop a strong trade network. Colonial lands that made up the New Netherlands were to be purchased in good faith from their rightful owners. Native Americans in the New York area responded initially with goodwill and acts of kindness. Many of the subsequent Dutch settlers and their leaders, however, acted far differently and exploited the Native communities, cheating them without even hiding their contempt for the people and arrogantly dismissing them as wild men.[6]

On February 25, 1642, Dutch governor William Kieft, in his continuing effort to expel Native Americans from the area of New Amsterdam, led soldiers on a night raid, repaying the Native Americans' kindness with a cruel slaughter. More than 120 men, women and children were mutilated and killed in their wigwams. According to Dutch reports, Native American women were cut open by the swords of the Dutch soldiers and babies bayoneted. Native American men had their hands cut off, and slashed children were thrown into the river to drown. The village was burned to the ground. The Dutch committee investigating the horror called it an "unnecessary, bloody and ruinous war."[7]

America's First Slaves

Contrary to common belief, the European colonial practice of importing slaves to North America under the guise of serving the advancement of God and country did not begin with the importation of African tribal people, but in fact began with the enslavement of the host people of this land.

Though there are many historical accounts, here are just a few occurrences of Native slavery:

In 1502, explorer Sebastian Cabot put on public display three Native Americans he had captured during his Arctic voyage.

At the dawn of the seventeenth century, Portuguese explorer Gasper Corte Real kidnapped more than 50 Native people and sold them into slavery. During this time, English expeditions sporadically attacked and kidnapped Native Americans along the eastern coast of the so-called New World.

In 1614, one of John Smith's captains captured a small group of Native Americans, took them back to Spain and sold them into slavery. John Smith himself advocated deception and intimidation toward Native people, recommending unrestrained violence to keep the tribes in line.[8]

During its formative stages, the new territory of Carolina began a systematic effort to enslave Native Americans, kidnapping or buying them to sell in the profitable slave trade with New England and the West Indies. Slavery actually became a central component of the Carolina economy during the early years of its development.

In Virginia in 1676, the assembly legalized the enslavement of Native Americans, paralleling the process Virginia followed in its enslavement of Africans. Enslavement was rationalized on the assumption that Native Americans were less-than-human, barbarous infidels whose population needed to be thinned out. In later years, it was often said that "gnats bred lice" in justifying the elimination of Native people as an obstacle to progress.[9]

The Puritans of New England punished the Pequot tribespeople for their opposition to European settlement by killing hundreds of Pequot men, women and children and selling hundreds of others into slavery. The captive male Pequots were sold and shipped to the West Indies, while the Puritans made domestic slaves of the tribe's women and children. This enslavement of Native Americans by colonists of Massachusetts Bay occurred at the very same time that the Puritans were attempting to organize a "holy" colony based on the dictates of the Bible.[10]

Many colonies, states and territories paid bounties for Indian extermination. Bounties varied from $25 to $130 for each male scalp and usually half that amount for a woman's or child's. "The only good Indian is a dead Indian" was a common expression that reflected the attitude that lasted 400 years. In 1775 the British Crown offered £40 for male Indian scalps and £20 for females' and children's.[11]

The Relocation Act

At the time my mother moved us from the reservation, the U.S. federal government was carrying out a policy of relocating Native people from their reservations to urban centers. The government subsidized the relocation of Native people to the cities through financial, housing and educational incentives, with the goal of assimilating them into the mainstream of American society. Behind this policy, the stated aim of which was to help Native people learn a trade, was the underlying goal of making Native people less of a burden on U.S. taxpayers. Like most attempts at legislated social engineering, the program was a dismal failure. Worse, it left Native people socially and culturally disenfranchised.

It was a noble scheme that in the end created more hardships, broke up more families and created more alcoholics for the skid rows of our major cities, including Oakland, Cincinnati, Chicago, Dallas and Minneapolis, among others. The program moved people to the city, put them through a quick training program, got them a cheap apartment, provided them with a short-term job and then left them stranded and lost in the worst parts of town. "Skin" bars in those cities became famous and were the most troubled businesses of that type. Quite a few of the uprooted Indian people finally lived and died on the streets.[12]

The well-meaning plan didn't work because the Indian people lost again—they lost family, children, language, ceremonies and a way of life. It worked for a few but hurt many.

Boarding Schools

The last Indian war was fought against Native American children in the dormitories and classrooms of government-sponsored boarding schools. Only by removing Indian children from their homes for extended periods of time, policymakers reasoned, could White civilization take root and childhood memories of a "savage" way of life gradually fade to the point of extinction—in the words of one official, "Kill the Indian and save the man."

The boarding-school era lasted roughly from 1875 to 1926, with the first such school being built in Carlisle, Pennsylvania, and the last in Riverside, California, in 1902. According to author David Wallace Adams, the prevailing theory was that Indian children, once removed from the savage surroundings of the Indian camp and placed in the purified environment of an all-encompassing institution, would slowly learn to look, act and eventually think like their White counterparts.[13]

Robert Ryan writes that these schools, often run by churches, existed to "educate the heathens and remove their pagan customs from their worship and language."[14] The sexual and physical abuse suffered by Indian children in these Christian boarding schools has been well documented in such books as *Wounded Warriors* by Doyle Abergast.

Many Native people across America have told me how painful it was to grow up in these schools without the benefit of seeing how a family lived, loved and worked together. They learned to live with each other the best way they could, which often involved a peer hierarchy where fighting was the norm and self-protection was the key to survival.

Many had their mouths washed out with soap or were physically punished for speaking their Native languages. One man told me the story of how he was tied to boiler-room heater pipes to punish him for speaking his language and to teach him to speak only English.

This was a tough life that many survived in a physical sense, but no one can measure the emotional wounding that took place. The process was inhumane; the results, harmful and predictable. Beautiful Native languages were demeaned and forgotten. Children did not see their parents and had no social models and little training to prepare them to later become fathers and mothers.

My mother grew up during the boarding-school era of U.S.-Native relations. She and her brothers and sisters and cousins attended St. Francis Boarding School on the Rosebud Reservation in South Dakota, a school run by Jesuit missionaries. My mother told me that some on the reservation wanted this education for their children, believing it was a way of survival for the future in the dominant White society. And for many Indian children the boarding schools did serve as an escape from the poverty, alcohol and abuse that was common in many of their homes, the result of the impoverished conditions created by the reservation system.

Some of these boarding schools still exist today. Unfortunately, they usually serve as a dumping ground for those young Indians who are considered problem children.[15]

Lynda's Story

Lynda, my friend and dear sister in Christ, was five years old in 1960. She remembers a man arriving one day in a small airplane at Tache Village where she lived. The man carried a clipboard and visited all the homes in her community. Soon after, she and many other children were taken for a ride in the plane to a place where buses were waiting to take them to a residential school near Fort Fraser, British Columbia.

When they arrived, Lynda and her brothers were separated; she would not see them again for a long time. She and the other girls were taken to a dormitory, where they all had their clothes removed and were showered. Each girl's hair was cut in exactly the same way, and they were given dress uniforms to wear. The girls were told they would not be called by their names anymore; instead they were given numbers. For the rest of the year Lynda was called "63."

Lynda remembers that one morning, when they were in the showers, one of the other girls was singing a hymn in her Native language. A nun came and dragged her out of the shower and began strapping her for speaking in her language. The little girl knew only a smattering of English and in her fitful state could plead only in her own language, asking why she was being punished. This provoked the nun to strap her even more. This incident planted in Lynda a seed of hatred toward White people and their religion.

At the school she was taught that all boys were bad and evil, creating in her a lasting distrust of men. She grew up fearful, closed off emotionally and bound up inside. She and the others were taught that God had made a mistake when He made them Indians and that this mistake was going to be corrected. And yet they were taught in religion classes that God was a God of love. Lynda grew up thinking this God of the White man was a very mean God indeed.

Only through the power and

love of God in Jesus Christ

can the First Nations

people be truly set free

and made whole again.

Lynda's story is not atypical among Native families. The residential schools that the children were carried off to created generations of emotionally scarred children, some of whom are still alive today, having grown to adulthood without the nurture and care of being raised by loving parents or other adult relatives. They grew up in a world of peer survival and abuse by staff members. These children later married and had children of their own, only to have their own children sent off to boarding schools. Today there are generations of dysfunctional people in many Native families whose difficulties can be traced directly back to the devastating influence of these boarding-school experiences.

The heartache and suffering of this kind of child abuse do not disappear with time. If not healed, they only grow worse. Only through the supernatural power and love of God in Jesus Christ can the First Nations people be truly set free and made whole again.

A PROPHETIC CALL

One day when my oldest son, Andrew, was eight years old, he spent several hours playing at the house of his friend Aaron, who is White. Later, after Andrew left, Aaron asked his mom and dad, "Did you know that Andrew Twiss is half Indian and half human?"

My wife, Katherine (who happens to be Caucasian), and I had a good laugh over this simple story of one boy's innocent attempt to describe the difference he saw between himself and his friend. It expresses poignantly the profound difficulty many people have in understanding those who are different from themselves. This anecdote only hints at the wounding those of us of Native heritage have suffered and the challenges that members of our lineage face in trying to find their place in an American culture quite different from their own.

When the heart is flooded with racial, cultural, ideological or denominational strife, there is little room in the heart to hold love, honor, respect and admiration for those who are different from us; we certainly find it difficult to recognize and admit our *need* for them. Yet perhaps at no other time in history have so many sensed an undeniable call from the heart of God to the entire Body of Christ to unite together across denominational, racial and ideological lines. Indeed, I believe there is a prophetic call from the heart of God to the Anglo church in America to recognize its historical and continued racism and indifference toward its Native brethren—and to make amends.

As I have the privilege to travel and to speak to Christian audiences across America, I constantly hear people saying they believe God is going to use Native people in a unique way to accomplish His sovereign purposes for our nation. The following vision captures this sense of expectancy that I encounter in God's people across the United States. David Tavernier, an Anglo brother, during a time of prayer and intercession had a profound experience with the Lord and recorded this message in October 1993:

> Finally, after many weeks of seeking the Lord, I simply asked, "Holy Spirit, what is the root sin in the heart of America?" Several days passed by and to my surprise the words "Native American Indians" began to resound in my heart. As I began to meditate on these words, something tremendous started to happen.
>
> Deep down on the inside of me I began to be burdened with grief. At first I had no idea why. I had no reason to grieve. I was deeply moved during periods of intercession to groaning, travailing (at times as in birth), weeping and actually mourning in the Spirit. For the next several weeks I was overwhelmed by an almost unbearable sense of loss, as though I had just lost a loved one. My heart was broken when I began to sense what must be the enormous depth of God's grief over the unchecked, unrepented sins of our forefathers and the devastation done to the Indians. It seemed as though I felt only a tiny portion of His sorrow, but even that was all I could bear.
>
> During this encounter the Lord opened my eyes and my heart and I began to understand with a deep bitterness of soul that generations past did not deal kindly with Indian people according to God's law of love and justice. It seemed the Lord showed me that the unchecked, unrepented sins of our forefathers have created a spiritual blockage hindering the move of God in our nation.

Centuries of humiliation and injustice have made them the most isolated, forgotten and deprived minority group in America. History shows there was a selfish, violent clash between our fathers and the Indians. As I prayed, the Holy Spirit made me aware that our ancestors were an aggressive people who overcame the less powerful Indian Nations with malice, anger, wrath, hatred, lying, covenant-breaking, deceit, fraud and trickery—all fueled by greed and self-righteous bigotry. Violence and abuse were repeated countless times to the degradation, destitution and wholesale destruction of Indian culture and people. Whole tribes were shattered and lost forever. Men who, with no fear of God before their eyes, shamelessly and without mercy exercised brutal power over them to satisfy their own sinful desires.

It was never the purpose of our Creator Father to crush the original inhabitants of the land in order to "manifest our destiny." This was done by sinful and arrogant men who acted apart from God, and it is the harvest from their sins that oppresses us today. In the book of Amos, God condemns all who make themselves rich and powerful at the expense of others. He holds nations, as well as individuals, accountable for their sin.[16]

The late President John F. Kennedy, in 1963, said:

Before we can set out on the road to success, we have to know where we are going; and before we can know that, we must determine where we have been in the past.

It seems a basic requirement to study the history of our Indian people. America has much to learn about the heritage of our American Indians. Only through this study can we as a nation do what must be done if our treatment of the American Indian is not to be *marked down for all time as a national disgrace* (emphasis added).[17]

I believe the Christian Native community must be recognized as a vital and integral part of the God-given destiny of America. We as a Church must ask our Creator Father to help us look back, repent and honestly seek reconciliation for the injustices of nearly five centuries imposed by Euro-American immigrants on the First Nations people of North America.

May we, by God's grace, work to see a different relationship between White and Native brethren in the next hundred years. May this also be true for indigenous peoples around the world. The cry of my heart is that the Church may be one in deed and truth, and that Native and indigenous people will find their God-given place in the Body of Christ throughout the nations!

The Navajo have a beautiful concept, *Hozho*, which roughly translated means, "being in harmony" or "walking in life with beauty." The Bible tells us that, because of sin, we all walk in darkness and disharmony, apart from God. No ceremony can take away the uncleanness of the human heart or make up for our inner unworthiness. Only Jesus can restore us to spiritual wholeness and harmony with God and life.

Native people have a rich spiritual and cultural heritage. It is into this reality that the Creator sent His Son. This was done in order to make a way for all people to once again travel the path of beauty and harmony that God the Father intended all His children to live in and walk in through Jesus Christ, the Waymaker. Jesus is our *chanku*—the way to God and to successful living. This is the Jesus Way.

CHAPTER TWO

THE SNAIL AND
THE RABBIT

One lazy, warm summer evening, a snail happily set out to visit his neighbor across the road. Distracted by the sights and smells of the languid evening and the beautiful colors of the sunset shining through the trees above, the snail failed to notice a turtle speeding along the well-traveled path. Before he realized what was happening, a terrific collision occurred. Later that evening in the emergency room, a police officer interviewed the snail for the accident report. When asked to give an account of the accident, the snail replied, "I don't remember a thing. It all happened so fast!"

Now, a rabbit had been watching this same incident from a little hill near the path. Even as the snail set out from his home, the rabbit immediately assessed the situation in his quick rabbitlike manner. After 15 minutes of seeing everything coming together, the rabbit left to get a bite to eat and then came back with his folding lawn chair to watch the final outcome. How the turtle and snail could actually let that happen to themselves was beyond the rabbit's ability to comprehend. In the mind of the rabbit, this was easily the most avoidable collision in the whole history of the animal kingdom. He could not fathom how two animals could be so stupid as to allow such a thing to take place. After all, if they had been normal like him, they quickly would have zigged and zagged, easily avoiding the whole thing. His only conclusion was, "Something is terribly wrong with them; they are abnormal creatures."

This story illustrates how differing perspectives affect our views of life and our perceptions of reality. To the snail, the turtle was a blazing rocket, while to the rabbit, the turtle's forward progress was barely perceptible. But whose definition of speed was correct?

Suppose that the world were populated only by snails, turtles and rabbits and that defining speed had become the pressing social issue of the day. Suppose rabbits made up 85 percent of the population, turtles 10 percent and snails only 5 percent. I would venture to guess that the more populous rabbits would prevail at defining the normal, socially correct point of view.

Now suppose the population were evenly divided into thirds. What then? Then suppose . . .

We all see and experience life and the kingdom of heaven differently. Our ethnic cultures as well as our experiences heavily influence how we perceive, define and interpret the world around us. Our worldviews are filters and lenses through which we see and focus, or take in, our world. Then, after our experiences have been filtered, we project our interpretations onto the world as though what we define to be normal, rational social behaviors are the *only* acceptable behaviors—for ourselves and everyone else.

Until mortality puts on immortality (see 1 Cor. 15:53), the kingdom of heaven on earth will be made up of "rabbits, snails and turtles" from every tribe, tongue and nation. The challenge is to know how to authentically esteem others as higher than ourselves (see Phil. 2:3), a task made especially difficult by the fact that various groups of people invariably set the standards and definitions for behavior—and they believe those rules, own them and become proud of them.

Each day the sun rises in the east and sets in the west. The rising sun signals the beginning of a new day, while at the same moment on the other side of the world, the setting sun is signaling the end of the day. One group is brushing their teeth and getting ready to start the day, while the other is brushing their teeth and getting ready to end theirs. Are they watching two different events? Are they viewing two different suns? It's the same event, the same sun. Why then does this singular event impact them in seemingly opposite ways? It has to do with the angle from which they are viewing the sun.

Likewise, our cultural worldviews (or, simply put, viewpoints) dynamically impact our interpretation of moral and social values. Divergent viewpoints can cause division and separation, though differing points of view are simply a comparison of how one group looks at life's experiences versus how another sees the same. Our distinctive viewpoints also affect our biblical hermeneutics (ways of interpreting) and applications of Scripture.

Which view of the sun's rising and falling is the more accurate? One or both—or neither?

THE EYE REALLY DOES NEED THE FOOT

Most missiologists agree that after 500 years of active missionary effort, only three to five percent of the Native population are born-again Christians. On some reservations the figure is less than one percent. When my wife and I lived on the Coeur d'Alene Reservation in northern Idaho in 1996, we did not know of one Native man (or more than a half dozen of women) who regularly attended any of the six evangelical churches located there. Unfortunately, the Coeur d'Alene tribe is not unique in this respect.

Christianity has not sufficiently or effectively penetrated Native culture. Not only have First Nations people not converted in great numbers, but the influence of believing Native American Christians has been all but absent from the evangelical mainstream in North America. In part this is due to the fact that, historically, non-Native Christians have made little genuine effort to find value in Native Americans or their cultures. Rather, the Native cultures have been labeled and denounced part and parcel as pagan, often occultic and definitely sinful.

In short, an authentic Native American cultural expression of Christianity has not been allowed to develop; the very idea has been rejected. Is it any wonder many Native people view Christianity as the White man's religion and blame Christians for the loss of their own culture and identity?

NATIVE LEADERS MISSING IN ACTION

The absence of First Nations Christians in key leadership roles in the evangelical mainstream in America today is one indicator that Native American believers have yet to be recognized as truly having anything of value to contribute to the Body of Christ.

Most of us can name any number of prominent African-Americans among national evangelical leaders: E. V. Hill, Tony Evans, T. D. Jakes, Joseph Garlington, Wellington Boone and many others. Luis Palau and Jesse Miranda are among a growing number of Hispanic evangelical leaders, and Ché Ahn is a rising leader from the Asian-American community. But how many Native American national, evangelical leaders can you name?

A number of spiritual leaders in America are known to be descended from Indian tribes: Oral Roberts and Kenneth Copeland from the Cherokee, James Robison from the Choctaw and John Sandford from the Osage, to name a few. But these men are recognized and honored as White men rather than Native Americans, having only a small degree of Indian blood. No religious leader of predominantly Indian descent is so well received and honored.

How often have you seen a First Nations leader pictured on the brochure of an upcoming ministry conference alongside any of the leaders mentioned above? Although not unheard of, sadly it is an almost nonexistent occurrence. Doesn't it seem reasonable to think that, after nearly five centuries of steady evangelism, at least two or three Native Americans would have emerged as significant leaders in the contemporary Church in America?

In a letter to the Corinthian church, the apostle Paul described the Church in terms of the human body, warning us against thinking that one part of the Body (person, people, organization, denomination, etc.) is more important or better than any other. He wrote, "The eye cannot say to the hand, 'I don't need you!' And the head cannot say to the feet, 'I don't need you!' " (1 Cor. 12:21, *NIV*).

It may be difficult to hear or to accept, but I believe that because of clashing cultural worldviews, the Anglo expression of Christ and His kingdom has said to the Native expression of Christ and His kingdom, "I have no need of you. I don't need your customs, your arts, your society, your language, concepts or perspectives." If you look at a thing and cannot identify any value in it, you will have no perceived sense of need for it. *And if you have no need for it, then you get along without it.*

Then, to add injury to insult, the Euro-Americans have said to the Natives, "But you need us. You need our theology, our leadership, our traditions, our economic resources, education, sciences, Sunday Schools—ultimately, our civilization."

Anglo Christians need to understand that these are some of the painful issues their Native brethren struggle with. Without understanding, there is no basis for compassionate change or for the possibility of partnership.

STILL JUST A MISSION FIELD

The Native community is to this day primarily viewed by Evangelicals as a needy but largely forgotten mission field, a group in need of *receiving* ministry. The flow of ministry between the Anglo and Native churches is almost always in a top-down direction, a one-way flow of goods, services, ministry and resources from the Anglo church to the "lower" Native church.

I would love to see some of our Anglo church leaders, when asked to help a Native church, say, "Yes, but on one condition: only if you will in turn send your pastors and leaders to come and equip us with the grace and gifting God has given you as Native people." When that day comes, it will verify that we are seen by our Anglo brethren as equal colaborers in the mission of the Church.

WE NEED ONE ANOTHER

An old Indian fellow was commenting one time on all the problems humankind struggles with as the result of Adam and Eve's disobedience and original sin. He said, "You know, if Adam and Eve had been Indians there in the Garden, we wouldn't have any of these problems with sin." He then explained, "If they had been Indians, they would have eaten that snake."

This humorous story points to the reality that the Anglo and Native segments of the Church need one another. Our different cultural and ethnic perspectives are the result of God's design and plan, not the devil's. Yet our awareness of our need for one another is sometimes dim, even nonexistent.

In all this time the non-Native evangelical community has yet to say to the Native American Christian community, "We need you." Why not? Because differing cultural worldviews determine how value is assigned, measured or determined, whether for a person, group or thing. The ethnocentric (based on the belief that one's own group is superior) and biased Euro-American worldview has greatly hindered the Church community's ability to see Native believers as valuable and necessary members of the Body of Christ. And wherever cultural or ethnocentric "oversight" is not acknowledged, cultural ignorance or mere insensitivity soon gives way to arrogance, spiritual pride and even disdain.

In Anglo culture it is said the squeaky wheel gets the grease: sought-for attention comes with increased vocal complaint. Historically, this remedy is foreign to Native thinking, as are many other White customs. But thanks be to our Lord, there is increasing grace in these days to speak of these things in a Christ-honoring, straightforward manner.

Addressing the tendency of Christian people to think of themselves as more important than they really are, Paul wrote in 1 Corinthians 12:22-26:

> No, much rather, those members of the body which seem to be weaker are necessary. And those members of

the body which we think to be less honorable, on these we bestow greater honor. . . . But God composed the body, having given greater honor to that part which lacks it, that there should be no schism in the body, but that the members should have the same care for one another. And if one member suffers, all the members suffer with it; or if one member is honored, all the members rejoice with it.

Allow me to point out five observations or applications based on this passage:

1. The apparent weakness of the Native church should not be a cause of neglect or rejection, but one of acknowledgment and of the assignment of importance, worth and necessity. Natives should be recognized as vital, equally important contributing members.

2. The presumed weaker members, the Native Christian community, are, at least biblically, deserving of even greater honor than that given those who are seen as strong, sufficient and important. For this honor to have value and significance to Native people, its expression needs to be legitimate, honest and pragmatic. We do not need more paternalistic tokenism in the guise of partnership, inclusion or empowerment.

3. Could it be that at this time in history God desires for the Church in America to give greater honor to those parts that lack it today? Many ministries, such as Promise Keepers, the National Association of Evangelicals, the Southern Baptist Convention and a growing number of denominations, have acknowledged their neglect of ethnic leadership and are now

beginning to emphasize the importance of the role of ethnic brethren.

4. God's providence is intended to produce in us a quality of concern and care for one another that truly reflects our heavenly Father's nonpartisan view of humanity.

5. In America today, the entire Church is suffering spiritually because of the suffering of the Native expression of the Body of Christ. We cannot escape our connectedness in Christ, and we must comprehend the Lord's requirement upon us to be more aware of the overall condition of the Body, not just those more prominent parts.

The Native condition is not merely a social issue; it is also deeply spiritual. It has strong ties to the past and has great bearing on the future fulfillment of God's intended purposes for our nation. The Body of Christ in North America cannot remain functionally healthy so long as it contains a detached, unattended appendage. We are all suffering as a result.

My primary concern for the role of Native peoples is not just for Native peoples themselves, but for the Kingdom. All people find their true value in the Kingdom. Our value as a people is determined by God's sovereign will and design, and His kingdom finds its value in its people—all of them.

All people find their true

value in the Kingdom.

NATIVE CULTURES EXIST
FOR A GOD-GIVEN PURPOSE

It is clear from Scripture that God is the creator of nations and the author of the flow of history—the first multiculturalist, so to speak. The very idea of culture began with God. The reformer John Calvin wrote concerning culture:

> The mind of man, though fallen and perverted from its wholeness, is nevertheless clothed and ornamented with God's excellent gifts. If we regard the Spirit of God as the sole fountain of truth, we shall neither reject the truth itself, nor despise it wherever it shall appear, unless we wish to dishonor the Spirit of God. . . . The men whom Scripture (see 1 Cor. 2:14) calls "natural men" were, indeed, sharp and penetrating in their investigation of earthly things. Let us, accordingly, learn by their example how many gifts the Lord left to human nature even after it was despoiled of its true good.[1]

Native cultures, as do all the cultures of man, reflect to some degree the attributes of our Creator. It is in Christ that we find the ultimate fulfillment of His holy and sovereign purposes for us as a people. If He has a unique role for us to play or a contribution to make in the fulfilling of His purposes for our nation in these days, then the Church must reconsider the place given to Native concerns in the evangelical mainstream in America.

ADAM AND EVE: THE FIRST INDIANS?

Genesis 2:7 says that "God formed the man [adam, meaning "image of God"] from the dust of the ground [adamâ, meaning "red soil"] and breathed into his nostrils the breath of life, and the man became a living being." So when God was preparing to make human beings, He first gathered together a pile of dirt—*red* dirt—and began to form a shape. (Remember, God said it was good dirt.)

So you can see from the Word of God that the first human beings created, Adam and Eve, may have been in fact *red-skinned* people! One might even say they were the first Indians.

As humans each of our bodies is made out of water and dirt—a little iron, zinc, magnesium, calcium, phosphate, etc. So, is one people's culture, biology or dirt better than another's, so far as God is concerned? Does He see red dirt as being better than brown, yellow or white dirt? No! All dirt is equal in His sight!

But because of the nature of our creation, we are more than dirt. We are living beings, created in the likeness and image of God (see Gen. 1:26). All people everywhere share this commonality as created beings of a supreme and loving Creator. Whatever it is that God is made of, that is the essence of our substance and existence.

John 4:24 says that "God is Spirit."

> God, who made the world and everything in it, since He is Lord of heaven and earth, does not dwell in temples made with hands. Nor is He worshiped with men's hands, as though He needed anything, since He gives to all life, breath, and all things. And He has made *from one blood* every nation of men to dwell on all the face of the earth, and has determined their preappointed times and the boundaries of their dwellings (Acts 17:24-26, emphasis added).

God made the world and everyone in it. From "one blood" God created all the nations—*ethnos* (ethnic groups)—of the world. Scientific experts are saying it can be proven genetically that all of humankind comes from one original set of genes. We are all descended from Great, Great Grandpa Adam and Great, Great Grandma Eve. There are not, biblically and scientifically speaking, different genes pools from which different races stem. Biblically speaking, there are no races of people. There is only one race of man—the Adamic race!

WHO IS GOD'S FAVORITE?

Although God sent His only Son to die for everyone (see John 3:16) and therefore loves all people equally, He did choose Israel for a specific purpose. That purpose was not to hoard God's blessings to themselves but to declare God's glory to the nations (see Pss. 67,87,96). Although God forbade the Israelites to allow themselves to be assimilated into the pagan cultures around them, He did not mean for them to isolate themselves from those nations and cultures. Sadly, God's chosen people often misinterpreted their calling as favoritism, thereby defeating the purpose for which God had chosen them.

In Acts 10 we read of two men receiving a divinely inspired vision from God: Peter, a Jewish man, and Cornelius, a Gentile man. Both experienced God speaking to them supernaturally in a trance or dream. Here is Peter's vision:

> He fell into a trance and saw heaven opened and an object like a great sheet bound at the four corners, descending to him and let down to the earth. In it were all kinds of four-footed animals of the earth, wild beasts, creeping things, and birds of the air. And a voice came to him, "Rise, Peter; kill and eat." But Peter said, "Not so,

Lord! For I have never eaten anything common or unclean." And a voice spoke to him again the second time, "What God has cleansed you must not call common." This was done three times. And the object was taken up into heaven again (Acts 10:10-16).

Soon after this vision, Peter spoke to a gathering of people at the house of Cornelius and said to them:

> You know how unlawful it is for a Jewish man to keep company with or go to one of another nation. But God has shown me that I should not call any man common or unclean. . . . In truth I perceive that God shows no partiality. But in every nation whoever fears Him and works righteousness is accepted by Him (Acts 10:28,34,35).

The *New International Version* expresses Acts 10:34,35 in this way: "I now realize how true it is that God does not show favoritism but accepts men from every nation who fear him and do what is right."

At the time, Jewish people were not to associate with people from other ethnic groups; it was socially and religiously forbidden. Peter had been brought up by his parents, extended family and community with a restrictive way of thinking about other nations. The Jewish people believed they were superior to others and fully believed this was the way God wanted them to think.

I believe the religious leaders of Israel, over time, had misinterpreted God's ultimate purpose to have a kingdom of priests. They erroneously concluded that God's purpose was to have a nation-state, a political body called Israel, as His singular human expression of His kingdom on earth.

But God spoke to Peter concerning a new way of thinking about his neighbors and others from the Gentile nations. Peter grasped the meaning of the vision and saw that God did not regard or look upon people with any sense of favoritism or partiality based on their nation of origin or cultural background. Peter, therefore, was no longer to show national favoritism or cultural egocentrism by regarding others in a condescending way or to refer to anyone in derogatory terms like "unclean" or "common." He learned that God accepts all men and women equally if they fear God and work righteousness.

THE GREATEST CHALLENGE

As I speak across the country, people ask me quite often what I think is the greatest problem among Native Americans. Is it alcoholism? Teen suicide? Unemployment? Gambling?

I believe the greatest challenge facing Native peoples is the unresolved anger, distrust, hatred and bitterness in our hearts toward Euro-Americans, based on centuries of injustice and oppression. I don't just mean the type of oppression committed by sinful nonbelievers; specifically, I'm addressing the injustice and rejection that have taken place within the family of God, the redeemed community of the Lord Jesus Christ, between Anglo and Native brethren. This is something the Word of God and the Holy Spirit call us to repent of and to correct. That means a fullness of repentance and restitution.

I am hoping there will be heard in the land, in our generation, a corporate crying out to God the Father in confession and repentance for our sins, seeking forgiveness and reconciliation. As Native people we must allow the Holy Spirit to help us deal with our unforgiveness, distrust and suspicion of our Anglo brethren in Christ. But without the confession of sin and the asking of forgiveness by Anglo brethren, the process for my people will be difficult (see Matt. 5:23,24).

Those who have suffered the most are the nonbelieving Native men and women who have been deprived, not only of economic well-being, but also of every vestige of true self-worth, because they do not know the love of Jesus who alone gives us all worth and dignity. Time after time, when efforts at reconciliation have taken place, I have witnessed Native people weeping because they finally feel affirmed by God.

When Anglo brethren have stood before their Native brethren and honestly, humbly and corporately confessed their neglect and rejection of them and then have spoken of how much they need them, the Holy Spirit has consistently released floods of forgiveness and healing. There has been a release of deep emotions, weeping and forgiveness. These times of reconciliation have become seedbeds for many genuine and long-term relationships between Native and Anglo brethren.

PREPARING THE NEXT GENERATION

What legacy are we leaving for future generations? Our children and grandchildren will grow up in a radically different America. Missiologists and sociologists alike use the expression "the browning of America." What will the ethnic complexion of America be in 25, 50, 100 years? It has been said that in the year 2030 the American population would be made up of equal parts Anglo/White and people of color. But by the end of the next century, if the Lord has not returned, the majority of the population will be largely brown. Anglo people will be a distinct minority of the population.

Peter underwent an unexpected and abrupt change of thinking regarding his view of people from cultural backgrounds different from his own. Have you looked into the Word of God and allowed the Scriptures to accurately reflect back to you what your attitudes and views should be toward others of different complexions and ethnic distinctives? The browning of society is not a possibility; it is a reality, not only in North America but also throughout the world. We will do our children a great disservice if we do not give them a solid biblical foundation upon which to build their lives as the world "browns up."

By understanding the beliefs and attitudes of people from different backgrounds, we can build honest and open relationships. Native people need to be understood as a modern people who have a rich heritage and history in this country.

THE IMPACT OF ETHNOCENTRIC ATTITUDES

"You know, Margaret, the grandchildren will be half-breeds." Only after we had been married a few years did we learn that, before our marriage, my future father-in-law had informed his wife of my Native heritage. He had seen the worst of Native people in the bars and on the streets of Fairbanks, Alaska, and had developed certain attitudes about them based on his experiences. Although both of my in-laws have since passed away, my father-in-law and I became very good friends, and all of us enjoyed our relationships together as a *tiyospaye*—an extended family.

Through the years I have heard what I refer to as attitudinal comments similar to that of my father-in-law, comments such as:

Why does the government keep building new homes for
    Indians? All they do is run them down and wreck them.
Why don't they get jobs like everyone else?
If Koreans and other immigrants can become so successful,

why can't Indian people do the same?
They're just abusing the system because they all get big casi-
no checks.

Comments like these reflect the ethnocentric notion that Native
people are unmotivated, lazy or lack personal ambition.

As we look at the attitudes between Natives and Whites, I think
it's important to understand what a powerful force the initial philosophy behind the U.S. government's reservation system was in
shaping the attitudes of most Americans today. The intent of estab-
lishing the reservations in 1887 was control: The reservations made
Native people dependent on the government for their existence.
Reservations became welfare states. Likewise, the government-
condoned slaughter of as many as 60 million buffalo in the 1870s
denied the Natives their primary source of food and helped to create a dependency mind-set among the tribes of North America.

Those who have lived for long under the oppression of a dominant culture often exhibit a victim mentality—a sense of deserved-
ness and a you-owe-me attitude. However, this mind-set is rapidly
changing among Native people as they have chosen new courses
toward self-government and self-determination.

Nevertheless, it is important to understand the significance of
prevailing attitudes. These attitudes are based on what people
believe and value—or devalue. The danger in beliefs and values is
not the beliefs and values themselves but the attitudes that
emanate from them. Superiority, arrogance, inferiority, subordi-
nation, trust, mercifulness and judgmentalism are a few examples
of attitudes stemming from our beliefs.

For example, a non-Native Evangelical might view a Native
person as having little ambition, avoiding work or being habitu-
ally late. The Native person in turn might view the Anglo-
American as a grasping, driving, insensitive materialist who

doesn't appreciate the environment around him or take time to sense and enjoy it.

Commissioner William Medill aptly expressed the conflicting viewpoints in 1848 when he said, "Apathy, barbarism and heathenism must give way to energy, civilization and Christianity; and so the Indian of this continent has been displaced by the European."[2]

People from one culture must take care not to alienate themselves from persons of another culture by harboring negative attitudes.

THE MAORI AND THE PAKEHAS

The Maori are the indigenous tribal people of New Zealand. They face the same issues as First Nations people face here in North America concerning attitudes from the dominant people group. In his book *One Faith, Two Peoples*, Lloyd Martin tells a story of these attitudinal issues:

> Many of the Waipuna leadership (Maori believers) were torn between their conviction that this was God's church (into which they ought to fit) and a growing sense of unease that maybe they didn't fit in. Faced with the seeming incompatibility of their faith and their culture, some began to drift guiltily back into their old lifestyles. Steve represented the feelings of the group at Waipuna to the leadership (Pakehas-Anglo brethren) and challenged them in terms of the new consciousness of racial issues sweeping the country.
>
> "You claim that we have a bicultural church, but we feel excluded from what you are doing."

"How can you feel excluded?" one leader asked. "Your group is represented on the leadership, you lead the worship in the evening service. The problem is that you people won't participate in the wider life of the church."

"Yes, we do need to make an effort," Steve admitted, "but what effort have you made to get to know us? All this time we have been coming to your church, but none of you have made an effort to come out and be part of what we are doing. You expect everything, including us, on your terms. We won't learn to work together until you make an effort to understand us. We understand you—we have to in order to survive. Everything we do together at the moment is based on your turf and your rules."

An effort was made by the church leadership to bridge the gap by inviting the Anglo folks to "camp out" over a Friday and Saturday in a traditional Maori community center, a Marae.

Over the next few weeks, however, reality set in. The process that they had hoped to start from the weekend died as the overall feeling from the wider church [Pakeha] was that "we've done our bit." Those who hadn't turned up . . . quietly pointed out to each other that the majority of the church was European and all this Maori stuff didn't have anything to do with "what we're supposed to be here for." [The group of people in the church] who believed there were demons in Maori carvings [and were critical of Maori culture] pointed to the rising consciousness of Maori issues and the exodus of Maori from the church as evidence that their culture was "pulling them away from the Lord."[3]

The attitude expressed by the Pakehas to their Maori brethren was that their own ways were normal and Christian, while the Maoris' ways were abnormal and unbiblical and, therefore, wrong or bad. In essence they were saying, "You need to change your ways and become like us." As a result, many of the Maoris reluctantly left the church, feeling there was no place for them unless they abandoned their culture. It is an example the Church would do well to study today in light of its desired evangelization of First Nations people.

CHAPTER THREE

A REDEMPTIVE VIEW OF NATIVE CULTURE

My wife's father was Norwegian and her mother Welsh, so Katherine looks very European. Needless to say, she and I are quite obviously from different "tribes." We had set up a tipi during an outreach in Portland, Oregon, and our son Ian, who was four at the time, spent the night with us. Katherine and Ian had had a busy day helping people set up their tipis, as several hundred Native people were staying in the encampment. As they were talking that evening, our son made a comment to her about how "White" his friend Johnny was.

Katherine said, "Well, Ian, I'm White, too."

Ian said, "No, you're not."

"Ian, look at my blonde hair and blue eyes and my skin color. I'm a White person just like Johnny."

Ian replied, "Mom, no, you're not! And you better stop saying that or I'm going to tell Dad! And he is going to spank your butt!"

Pretty strong words for a four-year-old, but surely they reveal that, to the young, race is not an external matter of color and appearance but something solely of the heart's attitudes.

This is a classic example of someone's defining reality from a personal prejudice and not by the facts. Regardless of the fact that Katherine is clearly Caucasian, Ian saw a Native woman. He was interpreting what he saw through the filter of his heart—his emotions.

Frequently, people approach much more serious issues in the same way.

Many issues can and often do hinder the Church's ability to carry out God's intentions on earth. Among these are prejudice and racial discrimination. Often these kinds of issues are seen as sociological problems. I would suggest, however, that if these issues bring division, distrust or schisms among believers and churches, then they are not merely social problems but Kingdom issues. And if they are Kingdom issues, they must be dealt with in a Kingdom manner.

DEFINING CULTURE

When looking at human cultures, we find there are many scholarly definitions and viewpoints about what culture is. This is a critically important subject if we are to understand the identity of Native people and their distinctive place in the Body of Christ. In this chapter I hope to present some points of view on culture to help us all to appreciate our differences better and to value them.

Rev. Adrian Jacobs of the Cayuga/Six Nations tribe is the founder and director of First Nations Centre for Ministry in Belleville, Ontario, Canada. Adrian and I have become close friends and associates, and I have come to greatly respect his views and wisdom. He was raised in the Handsome Lake Long House tradition of the Cayuga people before coming to Christ. As a result, he has some valuable insights to share concerning Christianity, culture and traditional religion. Much of what follows is adapted from a teaching by Reverend Jacobs entitled "Syncretism: The Meeting of the Two Roads" and is used with his permission.

Culture itself is neither good nor bad. One's cultural identity is intrinsically neutral—it helps define who one is as part of a people, tribe, tongue or nation. Simply put, culture is the normal or acceptable thinking or behavior for a group of people. One's cultural identity encompasses:

1. Social-kinship relationships
2. Language
3. Material things or objects
4. Aesthetic values—arts, music, drama
5. Religion or worldview
6. Economic systems
7. Political systems

All people, Christian or otherwise, respond to cultures different from their own in a variety of ways. Adrian Jacobs has identified several common responses of people toward those whose cultural expression is different from their own. One of these is *cultural blindness*. Though each of us is part of a culture, when one belongs to a dominant culture or is part of a cultural majority, he or she is often not aware of being part of a defined culture. When encountering someone different from themselves, the first reaction of those who are culturally blind is to classify the person as abnormal (with themselves, of course, serving as the measure for what is normal).

One time I was buying a car, and after being left alone for a time to consider the dealer's offer, the sales manager came back and said to me, "Well, Chief, did you make a decision yet?" I asked him if he had just called me a chief. He stammered a bit and apologized, saying he didn't realize I was a Native American. I then told him to give me a little more time to think about the offer. Two of my teenage sons were with me at the time and got a big kick out of the man's discomfort.

Another common response to those of a different culture is *cultural bigotry*. This is when someone remains closed minded, refusing to genuinely consider others' points of view while insisting that his or her own views are correct, superior or even godly.

In addition to blindness and bigotry, several other responses to differing cultural expressions can be found in the churches of America. These include:

1. *Absorption.* Pagan beliefs and idolatrous practices are overlooked or tolerated within a local church if the person holding these beliefs is a member in good standing. Such practices may even be allowed to coexist alongside the church.
2. *Syncretism.* This is the attempted union of different or even opposing principles or practices. The syncretist assumes that because two philosophies or religions are similar, they are in fact the same, or synonymous.
3. *Rejection.* The outsider's culture is dismissed as pagan and ungodly and is regarded as having little or no redeeming value. Many early missionaries responded to cultural conflict and the problem of the Indians' reverting to their old ways by isolating their converts from the rest of the "pagan" Indians and eliminating

anything that reminded them of their former culture. Many Natives through the centuries have been offended by the rejection of Indian culture as pagan because it strikes at the heart of who they are as a people. Attempts at forced assimilation of the Natives in the name of biblical evangelization in essence disqualified and devalued the worth of Native people, further distancing traditional Indians from Christians who have wanted to introduce them to Christ.

4. *Sanctification.* This is the proper biblical response to someone of a cultural background different from our own. Sanctification means setting something or someone apart for God's intended purposes. God wants Native believers to grow up into Christ and to judge their own culture by the light of God's Word. Whatever can be examined and is true to the Word of God is kept. Many Native cultural expressions are not a violation of the Word of God and therefore do not need to be abandoned. They can be redeemed and transformed into valid Christian behavior and usage.

My understanding of Adrian's teaching is this: By sanctifying people and their cultures, Jesus transforms them to become instruments of praise to His glory. Cultures without Christ are dead when they are separated from Him; to resurrect and transform these cultures is to make them alive or bring them to life as an expression of Himself. Cultures are to be instruments through which Christ reveals Himself to the nations.

All peoples are intended by God to find their value in the Kingdom. Our value as a people is determined by God's sovereign will and design. As created beings, we have a Creator; and though marred by sin, our cultures still carry some markings of the divine and holy nature of our Creator.

As Christians we do not represent only one culture in terms of ethnicity or nations of origin. The things we have in common as followers of the Jesus Way are supracultural. The fruit of the Spirit and the conduct and character that reflect a life committed to the Lord and His Word should be among the common features we share as followers of the Jesus Way.

Although we are incapable by nature of spiritual righteousness after the Fall, we are capable of civic virtue. The unregenerate man or woman is capable of understanding earthly things, but not heavenly things (see 1 Cor. 2:14). There are two reasons unbelievers can create just laws, good music and sound education. First, they are created in God's image; therefore rays of light still shine through. Second, God's common grace, exercised through His providential sovereignty, restrains wickedness, vice and ignorance from taking us to the depths to which they could.[1]

NATIVE CULTURE IS NO LESS GOD-GIVEN THAN ANY OTHER

Native culture, like all the cultures of man, reflects to some degree the attributes of our Creator Himself. It is in Christ that we find the ultimate fulfillment of His holy and sovereign purpose for us as a people. If He has a unique role for us to play or a contribution for us to make in the fulfilling of His purposes for our nation in these days, then as the Church we must reconsider the place in the evangelical mainstream in America that we give to Native expression.

Dr. Charles Kraft from Fuller Seminary writes:

> We see God working in terms of Jewish culture to reach Jews, yet, refusing to impose Jewish customs on Gentiles.

Instead non-Jews are to come to God and relate to Him in terms of their own cultural vehicles. We see the Bible endorsing, then, a doctrine we call *biblical sociocultural adequacy* in which *each culture is taken seriously but none advocated exclusively as the only one acceptable to God* (emphasis mine).[2]

If 97 percent of Native people are indeed dying without Christ, I believe we as Native Christians need to reexamine our methods and approach to bringing the gospel to Native people. Our approach must be more culturally relevant and therefore spiritually impacting.

Many times I have heard of Christian Native leaders who misinterpret and wrongly apply the Scriptures regarding culture. They exhort their fellow Native Christians to "come out from among them and be separate" and not to "touch what is unclean" (2 Cor. 6:17) in reference to our Native cultures, as if to say our cultures are evil and unclean. Yes, there *do* exist idolatrous and sinful practices that must be repented of; but the Word of God does not call us to turn away from being who God made us—Native people. When we come to Christ as First Nations people, Jesus does not ask us to abandon our sin-stained culture in order to embrace someone else's sin-stained culture.

Nowhere in the New Testament is there any call to believers to form a separate culture from the world; we were created to be separate from the world but never to leave it. So many believers have misinterpreted 2 Corinthians 6:17 as a call to leave the world. But what Paul is talking about is an internal, personal holiness, not a separate culture he wants us to create, as if simply living in it will make us holy. In forming our own Christian culture, all we have done is to leave the world without a witness from the inside, where we are supposed to be. When Native Christians reject the culture of their ancestors, Native people are left without a witness for Jesus Christ from within the cultural contexts of their spiritual, traditional and ceremonial life experiences.

Several years ago I attended some Native Christian meetings on a particular reservation. The camping area and meetings were adjacent to the central powwow grounds of their tribe. A number of the Christian Indians would not walk the several hundred yards to visit relatives or friends or even observe the powwow celebration because, in their view, Jesus had saved them out of "Egypt"; and they had no desire to return. They had been taught that many of their own cultural traditions were of the devil and should be avoided now that they were Christians.

Sadly, this perspective among Christian Natives is not a rarity or exception, but for many years has been the norm. In my opinion this is a most unbiblical and damaging perspective! And I am glad to report that a new perspective is steadily emerging.

THEY THANKED ME WITH TOBACCO

In May 1997 I spoke at a church in Merritt, British Columbia, and afterward was invited to share a traditional salmon dinner at the home of a Native family in a small subdivision owned by the Lower Nicola Band Council. When I arrived several families were sitting in the front yard. It was a beautiful spring afternoon, sunny and warm.

At the morning service that day, Kim, one of the ladies preparing the food, had given me a small package of tobacco. She had said it was the custom of her people to give tobacco as an expression of respect and honor. She had said she was grateful and was blessed by the message she had heard from me, her Native brother, and she wanted to bless me in the Native way. Should I have told her I couldn't accept her tobacco because smoking is sinful and giving tobacco is a pagan custom?

I had humbly thanked her for her kindness and generosity and had graciously accepted her special gift of tobacco. The tobacco represented for me the hope that we were beginning to touch Native people in some very deep and core areas of their cultural identity. The fact that she had felt comfortable enough to give the "preacher" a pouch of tobacco was a sign of unique trust and identity. I had been genuinely touched and deeply honored by this simple gift.

That afternoon following a delicious meal, Kim's husband, Cedric, brought out dessert for us to enjoy. It was a kind of porridge made of local Saskatoon berries, pieces of bitterroot and small salmon eggs—different, but tasty. Afterward, as we enjoyed the sunset in the cool of the evening, we discussed the morning service. I asked if they had ever heard anyone teach that their cultural expressions could be used to praise and worship Jesus Christ. Some of the family members had been Christians for 20-plus years, but they answered, "Never." They said they had been taught by Native and non-Native church leaders alike that their cultural expressions were bad and demonic and needed to be rejected. I was the first they had heard teach from the Bible that God wanted to set them free to express their love and devotion to their heavenly Father through their unique cultural expressions of music, singing, dance, language and worship. And they were so thankful.

I sometimes feel sad, other times angry, that our people have been so victimized by bad Bible teaching. Gross misapplications of Scripture have in many ways robbed and deprived Native believers of their God-given expressions of praise to God. The freedom promised by the Word of God—and so desperately needed—is often replaced by a destructive, ethnocentric interpretation of Scripture, leading to more fear and bondage rather than freedom and liberation.

This family shared with me how, at times they felt ostracized from their people because they attended church. This was not because of their faith in Christ but because the church had taught them that they should separate themselves and no longer participate in the traditional social activities of their people. They were caught between the church and their people—the unnecessary tension between being a Christian and being Native. This is the theological dilemma and inconsistency that many of us feel called to address and bring biblical correction to in the Native work.

They were caught between the church and their people—the unnecessary tension between being a Christian and being Native.

At the conclusion of our time together, the family began making plans to hold a series of Christian meetings in the band council building and even in the community's powwow dance arbor. I love to see Native believers set free by God's Word to consider new and different ways to impact their people for the glory of almighty God.

FEAR OF EVIL OR FREEDOM OF TRUTH

I readily acknowledge that when attempting to redeem cultures—sorting out the usable from the unusable—there is a need to be cautious so that we do not cross the line into syncretistic practices that combine idolatrous or occultic spiritual ceremonies with Christian ways and doctrines. At the same time I do not want fleshly fear to be a primary deterrent to discovering a more Native cultural expression of our Christian faith. Scripture clearly states that fear is not of God and actually brings torment to our lives (see 1 John 4:18).

My Samoan friend and founder of Island Breeze Ministry, Sosene Le'au writes:

> God wants us to go on the offensive. Jesus said that the gates of hell will not prevail against His church (Matthew 16:18). Jesus does not say that the gates of the church will be able to withstand Satan's assault. He turns it around and says that the gates of hell will not be able to withstand our assault. The idea is that Christians will crash through the gates of hell to set free those who have been held captive for so long. This is what cultural redemption is all about.[3]

Christian Native people have been given the Spirit of the Lord, bringing power, love and a sound mind (see 2 Tim. 1:7). Nevertheless, for far too long they have been taught to be afraid of their own culture. I am firmly convinced that if our hearts beat with the Father's heart to reach lost people, if we walk in council with wise brothers and sisters, if we remain humble, then even if we do inadvertently cross the line, the Holy Spirit is big enough and sufficiently powerful to correct any possible errors and to transform our worst blunders into the best wine for the feast (see John 2:1-11). This does not give us license to be careless or flippant, but it should reassure our hearts that we are free to venture in Him.

Religion is often defined as man's searching for God; true Christian *faith* is God's searching for and finding man. Religion is a striving to please God, fearful of failure and condemnation; faith is God's pleasing man, filling us with His love and acceptance. Religion continually makes up rules by which to measure and judge one another; faith heals a man's withered hand on the Sabbath, lets a wicked woman wash the Master's feet unafraid of defilement, and eats with publicans and sinners.

I believe the Holy Spirit is teaching us today to love and accept one another far beyond what our petty rules and traditions have taught.

THE CHIEFS SPEAK

What follows are two historic speeches from Native chiefs that capture the unique style or flavor of Indian thinking. Representing two early responses of Native leaders to Christianity, these insightful speeches reveal (1) a willingness to believe, befriend and trust White people and their new religion and (2) a seeming inability of Christians to communicate cross-culturally, leaving a people still questioning and lost. Many of the issues raised by these chiefs more than a hundred years ago still exist in the Church today, and we are still wrestling with them.

Chief Spotted Tail

The Brule chief Spotted Tail (Sinte-Gleska) at first counseled his tribe to accept the White man's way of life. But many questions disturbed him as over the years he observed the Whites' contradictory behavior and broken promises. His people had been approached successively and converted by several groups of

Christians, each of whom insisted the Brulés follow the only right way of life. One day, Spotted Tail questioned Capt. G. M. Randall of the 23rd U.S. Infantry, whom the Indians called Black Beard, about the contradictions the chief had noted in Christianity:

> I am bothered what to believe. Some years ago, a good man, as I think, came to us. He talked me out of all my old faith. And after a while, thinking that he must know more of these matters than an ignorant Indian, I joined his church and became a Methodist. After a while he went away. Another man came and talked and I became a Baptist; then another came and talked and I became a Presbyterian. Now another one has come and wants me to be an Episcopalian. What do you think of it? . . .
>
> All these people tell different stories, and each wants me to believe that his special way is the only way to be good and save my soul. I have about made up my mind that either they all lie, or that they don't know any more about it than I did at first. I have always believed in the Great Spirit, and worshiped him in my own way. These people don't seem to want to change my belief in the Great Spirit, but to change my way of talking to him. White men have education and books, and ought to know what to do, but hardly any two of them agree on what should be done.[4]

Chief Red Jacket

After a missionary addressed his tribe at a meeting in Buffalo, New York, in 1805, Chief Red Jacket of the Iroquois responded, saying:

Friend and brother, it was the will of the Great Spirit that we should meet together this day. He orders all things, and he has given us a fine day for our council. He has taken his garment from before the sun, and caused it to shine with brightness upon us; our eyes are opened, and we see clearly; our ears are unstopped, and we have been able to hear distinctly the words that you have spoken. For all these favors we thank the Great Spirit and Him only. . . .

Brother, listen to what we say. There was a time when our forefathers owned this great land. Their seats extended from the rising to the setting sun. The Great Spirit had made it for use by the Indians. He had created the buffalo, the deer, and other animals for food. He made the bear and the beaver, and the skins served for clothing. He had scattered them over the country, and taught us how to take them. He had caused the earth to produce corn for bread.

All this he had done for his Red children because he loved them. If we had any disputes about hunting grounds, they were generally settled without the shedding of blood.

But an evil day came upon us; your forefathers crossed the great waters, and landed on this island. Their numbers were small; they found friends, not enemies; they told us they had fled from their own country for fear of wicked men, and came here to enjoy their religion. They asked for a small seat; we took pity upon them, granted their request, and they sat down among us. We gave them corn and meat; they gave us poison in return.

The White people had now found our country, tidings were carried back, and more came among us; yet we did not fear them. We took them to be friends; they called us brothers, we believed them, and gave them a larger seat. At length their numbers had greatly increased, and they wanted more land, they wanted our country. Our eyes were opened and our minds became uneasy. Wars took place; Indians were hired to fight against Indians, and many of our people were destroyed. They also brought strong liquor among us.

Brother, our seats were once large, and yours were very small. You now have become a great people, and we scarcely have a place left to spread our blankets. You have our country, but you are not satisfied; you want to force your religion upon us.

Brother, continue to listen. You say that you are sent to instruct us how to worship the Great Spirit agreeably to His mind, and if we do not take hold of the religion which you White people teach, we shall be unhappy hereafter; you say you are right and we are lost. How do you know this to be true? We understand that your religion is written in a book. If it was intended for us as well as for you, why has not the Great Spirit given it to us, and not only to us, but why did He not give us, and our forefathers, the knowledge of that book, with the understanding it rightly? We know only what you tell us. How shall we know to believe, being so often deceived by the White people?

Brother, you say there is but one way to worship and serve the Great Spirit. If there be but one religion, why do you White people differ so much about it? Why not all agree as you can read the book? . . .

Brother, the Great Spirit has made all of us, but he has made a great difference between his White and Red children. He has given us a different complexion and different customs. To you he has given the arts; to these he has not opened our eyes. We know these things to be true. Since he has made so great a difference between us in other things, why may we not conclude that he has given us a different religion according to our understanding? The Great Spirit does right. He knows what is best for his children. We are satisfied.

Brother, you now have heard our answer to your talk. As we are going to part, we will take you by the hand, and hope the Great Spirit will protect you on your journey, and return you safe to your friends.[5]

The chiefs and other Indians drew near the minister, but he arose hastily from his seat and told them, "There can be no fellowship between the religion of God and the works of the devil!" He could not shake their hands. After this incident Chief Red Jacket became one of the fiercest opponents of the White man and his ways.

LET THIS MIND BE IN YOU

These views of these two great chiefs capture the failure of one people to legitimately try to understand, value and make room for another people of another culture, all in the name of God. The real issues had little to do with God or the Bible. The real issues stemmed from clashing worldviews, cultural biases and prejudices and an unwillingness to choose the path of humility—an unwillingness to esteem others of different cultures as though higher than themselves (see Phil. 2:3). This was hubris (spiritual pride) in the name of and for the cause of Christ.

Spotted Tail and Red Jacket call to us from out of the past and challenge us to choose the higher road—to choose the Jesus Way above denominational ways, above racial ways, above political ways, above nationalistic ways. I believe the Word of God challenges us to look beyond the things that are seen with the natural eye (see 2 Cor. 4:16-18) and not to make harsh judgments based on issues that soon will pass away.

Paul wrote, "Let this mind be in you which was also in Christ Jesus" (Phil. 2:5). Jesus made the greatest cultural leap of all time just for us! He gave up and left behind the unlimited joy of paradise—the "culture" of heaven—to be born into human culture. He left the daily face-to-face fellowship with the Father to face the frailty of sin-marred human relationships, knowing that His new friends would disclaim and abandon Him and that one of His closest associates would betray Him for a mere 30 pieces of silver.

Jesus was the ultimate and perfect example of cross-cultural ministry.

CHAPTER FOUR

A NATIVE WORLDVIEW

As we have seen, most non-Indians have been unable to discern value in Native cultural expressions of Christianity and therefore have seen no need to include these Native expressions with their own. I now want to show, as clearly as I can, how many Native cultural viewpoints are in fact quite biblical, valuable and even necessary for the life and growth of the Church in North America today. I will look at several of these distinctive Native viewpoints and endeavor to show how they can make a positive contribution to the spiritual life and growth of all in the Church.

> Once there was an Indian who became a Christian. He became a good Christian; he went to church, and he didn't smoke or drink, and he was good to everyone. He was a very good man. Then he died. First he went to the Indian hereafter, but they wouldn't take him because he was a Christian. Then he went to heaven, but they

wouldn't let him in—because he was an Indian. Then he
went to hell, but they wouldn't admit him there either,
because he was so good. So he came alive again, and he
went to the buffalo dance and the other dances and
taught his children to do the same thing (Anonymous).[1]

For many tribes their ideal condition is something akin to
the *shalom* of the Old Testament: peace, prosperity, security and
well-being. As I mentioned, the Navajo have a word or concept
called *Hozho*, which roughly means "walking in beauty" or
"walking in harmony." The Navajo believe harmony is the perfect way to live in this world. When things go wrong—sickness,
disasters, communication of human problems—it is because
someone is out of harmony and no longer walking in beauty.
Ceremonial "sings" and sand paintings are then performed to
restore a person to Hozho.

Jesus Christ is the Shalom of God. For those of us who are in
Christ, there is true freedom, forgiveness, power and ability to
walk in the joy and beauty of the Lord, who alone is our High
Priest. He is the only one who can cleanse, heal and restore us to
God the Father's heavenly Hozho. Repentance, confession and
forgiveness are thus the means to restoration.

The comparisons that follow—though admittedly somewhat
unbalanced—are not intended to represent Native perspectives as
being better than White perspectives but as equally valid. I believe
a consideration of these perspectives will benefit your spiritual life.

THE NATURAL AND THE
SUPERNATURAL: NATIVE PEOPLE DO
NOT HAVE A SPLIT VIEW OF REALITY

One of the ideas that is expressed again and again by Native cultures is that their sacred ways are inseparable from the ordinary.

Most evangelical Christians, whether they realize it or not, have compartmentalized worldviews, whereas most Indian people have *integrated* worldviews.

Western culture tends to compartmentalize life. Religious activity is often kept separate from all other areas, making religion just one segment of life. For Native people religion is a way of life.

In Western mentality there is the sacred and the secular, a natural versus spiritual split of reality. This split view originates not in true Hebraic-Christian faith but in classic Greek philosophy, in which man and his intellect are considered to be at the center of the universe.

This conflict between the integrated worldviews of the Indian and the compartmentalized worldviews of most Western Evangelicals has been among the greatest hindrances to effective communication between the White man and Native people. It has also proven a tremendous obstacle to the growth of Native people who profess faith in Jesus Christ, for to them it means they must abandon their entire approach to community and spirit to accept a way that feels foreign and unnatural to them.

Gnosticism

I feel it is critically important to have a basic understanding of the historic philosophic roots that led to the Western culture's segregated, or dualistic, view of reality. This dualism has its roots in an ancient Greek philosophy called gnosticism, which has greatly—and negatively—impacted the ability of Euro-Americans to value Native cultural expressions.

The word "gnosticism" is derived from the Greek word *gnosis*, which means "knowledge or right knowledge." Gnosticism is the teaching or belief that you're saved by right knowledge. Christian author John Fisher writes:

> Gnostic Christians believed that there was a distinct separation between the material and spiritual worlds. The spiritual world was the only one that mattered, since it was the seat of knowledge and contained the ultimate truth. The material world was an illusion and not to be trusted.[2]

What Western Christians struggle with, then, is a dualistic belief that for God to be *in* something, that thing must transcend the ordinary—it must become outwardly different in order to distance itself from the natural, evil world and thus become "Christian." They cannot accept a natural expression of God among us. This is in absolute contradiction to what the Bible teaches in John 1:14: "And the Word [God] became flesh and dwelt among us."

So how has this ancient philosophy affected missions among tribal people? Let's look again at what John Fisher has to say:

> The Gnosticism of today is not much different: Believe the right things about God and do as you please. Christians don't actually admit to this as a life philosophy, of course, but it is what many of us do. *We have been trained in the nuances of thinking with a split mind.*
>
> Are these the only options—to live in two worlds in either frustration or cultural schizophrenia, or to remain insulated in the small safe zone that rings us with a Christian sub-culture [as defined by Euro-Americans]. In the first, Christianity fills only a portion of a believer's existence; in the second, it may take up

more of one's life, but reality is reduced to that which can carry the "Christian" [Anglo] label.

Our confusion about the world and our place in it begins with how we think about the world and our place in it. Since we are products of our culture as well as of our faith, we must be prepared to look in both directions (emphasis mine).[3]

So, you see, the North American Native's integrated view of life and spirituality is actually much closer to the classic Hebraic-Christian view of life than is the contemporary Western evangelical's segregated view.

What this gnostic influence has left us is an artificial and less-than-biblical separation of Native/natural/earthly culture from Christianity—almost as though a circumcision, or cutting away, of Native culture has taken place. In the Early Church, Paul was constantly dealing with the misguided notions of Judaizers, who wanted to require that all new male Gentile believers become circumcised in order to be saved. They wanted to impose a cultural practice on other people as part of their salvation. Paul went toe-to-toe with Peter in a public meeting to refute the erroneous and damaging belief that required Gentile believers to adhere to Jewish law.

Wakan Tanka, the Great Spirit

Contrary to popular belief, not all Native beliefs are spiritistic, pantheistic or animistic. Most North American tribes were in fact monotheistic, believing in one universal, absolute being who furnished moral guidelines for their conduct and who motivated every living thing. The Lakota/Sioux called him *Wakan Tanka*, or "Great Spirit."

Someone with a gnostic Greek or Western worldview, when confronted with the biblical account of Balaam's talking donkey (see Num. 22:28-30), would question whether or not a donkey could actually talk. Because we know donkeys can't talk, it must then be assumed that the author was not speaking literally but metaphorically or allegorically. However, the classic Hebrew or Native would be more concerned with what the donkey had to say, rather than whether or not she could actually talk.

An American Indian would not have been especially surprised had a tree spoken to him, like the burning bush that spoke to Moses. A Native's belief was integrated into his daily life, with the Creator always present and manifest in all things. However, many Christians would say that any Native who believes a tree can talk must be practicing animism, spiritism or pantheism, although Jesus spoke directly to the winds and the waves and they heard Him and obeyed (see Luke 8:24,25).

Instead of dividing our lives into sacred/spiritual and secular/natural compartments, as Christians we would all benefit by seeing our faith as central to everything we do. We would stop viewing our employment situations as secular, non-religious work and Sunday mornings as our spiritual activity. Jesus has called us to be His followers 24/7—every hour of the day, every day of the week. We are spiritual beings living in this physical world.

NATURE: WE ARE PART OF CREATION, NOT SUPERIOR TO IT

It goes without saying that Native people are human beings; but that has not always been believed by our White brothers, who often regarded us as non-persons. "Human beings" is a traditional term that many tribes use in describing themselves. It distinguishes us from the four-leggeds, the winged ones and other creatures but does not necessarily make us superior to them.

Native Americans see themselves as a part of the whole creation. They have long perceived and pursued a balanced relationship between man and the environment—a partnership of equality and respect.

The Euro-North American view of nature places man as master over nature. Much of this view is based on an interpretation of Genesis 1:28:

> Then God blessed them, and God said to them, "Be fruitful and multiply; fill the earth and subdue it; have dominion over the fish of the sea, over the birds of the air, and over every living thing that moves on the earth."

Misinterpretation, misapplication and abuse of this passage has resulted in the rape of the land and the senseless and willful destruction of animals according to the whims of man, rather than inspiring responsible stewardship of God's creation. Natural resources have been exploited, restructured and manipulated in the service of humanity, without respect to the will or purposes of God. Nature is thought of as having neither will nor desire, though Romans 8:19-21 (*NIV*) seems to implies that it has all three:

> The creation waits in eager expectation for the sons of God to be revealed. For the creation was subjected to frustration, not by its own choice, but by the will of the one who subjected it, in hope that the creation itself will be liberated from its bondage to decay and brought into the glorious freedom of the children of God.

According to the Western mind-set, all that is contained within the universe consists of inanimate objects to be used, and the universe itself is but a place for man to carry out his desires and wishes through the powers of science and technology.

The Western industrialized world and postmodern society failed to realize until it was almost too late that nature must be respected and preserved. As far back as can be traced, Indian people have been aware of this need. For the most part, Native people have respected nature, killing only what they needed for food, clothing or shelter. Natives believe the land was created by God and, hence, is sacred, while Western culture views land as a natural resource or commodity.

To this day one of the major sources of conflict between Euro-American and Native culture is land. The land-claims issue goes further and deeper than a desire to obtain more land or big checks. To the Natives the land is sacred, given by the Creator to be cared for and loved.

Many Evangelicals have a poor biblical understanding of nature and take a flimsy political position on the environment. I venture to state that the Native American perspective is much closer to the ancient Hebrew understanding of creation and is a much more holistic and integrated view. Should the Lord not return soon, the Church will surely have to think through these environmental issues if our children and grandchildren are to survive another hundred or more years.

TIME: QUANTITATIVE OR QUALITATIVE?

To the Euro-American time is quantitative; but to the Native American it is qualitative, as evidenced by the older Native man who was living on a reservation. When asked if he had lived on the reservation all his life, he replied, "No, not yet."

I was talking with my Maori friend Monte Ohia of New Zealand one afternoon about the way indigenous people think about time. He related the following story of his visit to South Africa among the Zulu people. He and his host were driving to a meeting where Monte was to speak. When Monte asked what time the meeting was scheduled to start, his host said in about half an hour. When Monte asked him how far away they were from the town where the meeting was to be held, his host said about an hour. When they arrived more than an hour late, all the people were waiting as though nothing was wrong. His host told Monte, "Don't worry about it. The White people have the clocks and the watches, but our people have the time."

A word to describe one of the major qualities of time among the Indians is "appropriateness." An event begins when it is appropriate. Most Indian languages do not even have words to designate time. In Western cultures, however, time is regarded as a commodity. Americans sell it, buy it, borrow it, waste it, kill it, make it up, take it and, if we run afoul of the law, do it. As Americans we are obsessed with time.

To the Native person, his or her priority is the significant thing he or she is doing right now. According to the Western worldview, what I am doing right now is subject to what I have to do in one hour. The present is subject to the future. In the Native view what I need to do in one hour is subject to what I am doing right now. The future is subject to the present.

Whose definition of time will turn out to be the correct one, the biblical one? And is it an either/or situation?

Native people have a *circular* view of time as opposed to the Westerners' *linear* one. To the Westerner time is like a flat line and moves from one end to the other. This linear view separates time and life into three categories: past, present and future. To the Native, however, everything is eternally connected because time is a continuous, unbroken circle. Native people's history has a lot to say about the present and future because our identity is forever connected to our past.

So many of us are ruled by our DayTimers, calendars and appointment books. If church on Sunday mornings goes beyond the allotted time, we begin to lose interest. I am not saying that the Native concept of time is better, only that it is equal in both value and importance and worth considering as an option. In the nineteenth century there were no wristwatches; White men carried pocket watches. Some Plains Indians said, "White man carries his God in his pocket," because he never did anything without consulting it!

IDENTITY: A STRONG SENSE OF BELONGING

Traditional Native culture has always emphasized the submission of individuality to corporate identity—seeing ourselves as one of the people. No one person is to rise too far above the others without giving back to the community. The strength of the tribe and its ability to survive depends upon perceived and acted-out solidarity. One of the great challenges for the Church has been to effectively communicate to Natives the Western individualistic gospel and emphasis on personal growth in the Christian life within the context of the Natives' strong connection to family, tribe, clan and people.

The reason many Native young people have found it difficult to succeed off the reservation is their strong connection to home. (In the Anglo culture this is often viewed as an indication of personal weakness, a lack of intestinal fortitude.) Native people possess a strong sense of belonging to the greater community. An individual decision for Christ may threaten the integrity of the group and may cause expulsion of that individual, because the decision is viewed as being for the welfare of the individual rather than the whole tribe.

Our greatest strength as the

Body of Christ is this:

Though we are different

individuals, we are

one in Him.

When a convert to evangelical Christianity is faced with a demand to reject traditional tribal, spiritistic practices, that person often appears to the community to be rejecting his or her community, family and friends. To the individual-oriented Westerner, Native attachment to corporate decision making is not fully understood and, therefore, is not taken into account when introducing Christianity to Native social structures. Because of their loyalty and sense of belonging to the tribe, it is very difficult for Native individuals to stand against familial pressure, make a unilateral decision for Christ and stick to it.

The Bible is replete with admonitions and commands to see ourselves and live our lives as connected members of the Body of Christ. Our personal lives as followers of the Jesus Way should reflect a quality of love and unity seen only among God's people. Jesus said, "By this all men will know that you are my disciples, if you love one another" (John 13:35, *NIV*).

I believe this is a significant and powerful point of view that, if subscribed to, would strengthen our Christian experience as the Body of Christ. So often our provincial allegiance is to our denomination, tradition or local church. When this becomes out of balance or extreme, we miss out on the fact—and huge blessing—that we are part of something much bigger.

Our greatest strength as the Body of Christ lies in the fact that though we are different individuals, we are one in Him. We must regain what Natives have never lost: the understanding that our togetherness is more important than our individuality, that we are members one with another.

As a Christian man my personal sense of identity lies within my corporate belonging as part of God's *ecclesia*, or "called-out ones."

THE IMPORTANCE OF POWER

Perhaps the most important element in the way North American Native peoples have long viewed life is the concept and acquisition of power. Nothing could be accomplished without it. With power, it was believed, anything was possible. A bountiful harvest, a successful hunt, a healthy birth—these and countless other activities and accomplishments of living were predicated on the possession of power. Conversely, those individuals who failed in their activities and suffered misfortune were thought to lack power.

This very concept implies belief in a creator. All Native cultures have a supernatural orientation—the idea of a Native atheist would be an oxymoron! Concerning sickness, most tribal peoples ask, "Who caused this?" rather than "What caused this?" Western man confronts an "it," while the North American Native confronts a "thou." What makes the universe a thou is the presence of power. Power is the life force of the universe; without power there would not have been creation. In the Bible we read:

> And He is before all things, and in Him all things hold together (Col. 1:17, *NASB*).

This is an apt description of power as perceived by Native people.

A growing number of traditional Native Americans believe that their current social, economic and spiritual condition is the result of failing to continue the tradition of performing power-generating rituals. The function of power is to provide the individual or group with sufficient supernatural energies to survive in a mysterious and modern world. Consequently, there is a strong move among Natives to restore many of the traditional ceremonies, the most prominent of these being the Sun Dance. Not only is there a powerful pan-Indian renaissance of Native spirituality sweeping across North America today, but similar movements are appearing among indigenous peoples worldwide.

We must help Native people to see that the Christian faith is the only real and working power of God for today—that Jesus Christ is not only about eternal reward but *shalom* for this life also.

I believe that one of the greatest problems faced by early missionaries was that Jesus Christ did not replace the traditional power core of Indian beliefs. In a great many cases, He was simply added as another source of possible power alongside others.

In other cases, Native people displayed acquiescence in form but not in substance. As has become all too common in every quarter of society, visiting evangelists and missionaries have led people to Christ with a salvation prayer and then left, thinking they had completed their job. But without discipleship there is incomplete repentance and incomplete renewal of the mind (see

Rom. 12:2). If the name and person of Jesus Christ does not become the new center of the convert's worldview in place of his former reliance on impersonal power from an impersonal deity, then repentance and transformation are incomplete.

A very large number of Native people today, in spite of having a Christian label, have far more faith in their traditional rituals to bring them peace, happiness and success than they do in the rites of the Church. (I think, though, that most have fear *of* the spiritual world rather than faith *in* it.)

The Lord Jesus Christ will not take His place fully at the center of the Native worldview until He is perceived as the only free source of power, able to save completely, not just sometime in the future but now—meaningful, powerful and effective for the living of life moment to moment and not merely saved from sin to escape hell *after* this life.

NUCLEAR FAMILY VERSUS EXTENDED FAMILY

In Western culture, emphasis is placed on the nuclear family: dad, mom, brothers, sisters and grandparents. In Native culture, the extended family is given great importance: father, mother, brothers, sisters, grandparents, uncles, aunts, cousins, nieces, nephews and in-laws. In traditional Lakota/Sioux culture, each individual enjoyed the security of belonging to the *tiyospaye*, or "extended family." Though this is no longer what it once was, it is still a highly valued and vital reality in Lakota social structure. The same can be said for most Native cultures. Even today, roughly 40 percent of Indian households on the Pine Ridge reservation in South Dakota are composed of multiple nuclear families.

The kinship system of Native culture is vastly different from the idea of family in mainstream Anglo-American culture. Aunts, uncles and cousins are all integral parts of a Native person's family. When I meet someone from near my childhood home in South Dakota, one of the first things we ask each other about is our relatives. We learn about people by knowing who their relatives are.

Natives are very mindful of the fact that historically they have not had to be reminded to feed the hungry, clothe the poor or give shelter to those in need. For the most part they do it instinctively, sincerely and with pleasure. They visit the sick and afflicted and are sympathetic to those who suffer misfortune or disaster. Why? Because among Indian people, your neighbor is your relative. In this way the Native tradition is a strong portrait of the biblical reality of our oneness in Christ as the extended family of God—a true picture of the Body of Christ.

Among the Lakota/Sioux, *mitakuye oyasin* is a term of greeting to a gathering of people, which roughly translated means "all my relatives" or "all my relations." Traditionally this was a way of acknowledging our ties to and respect for the creation all around us and the audience we were addressing. We say among ourselves we are *oyate kin*, "the people." This is also how most other tribes of First Nations people think of themselves: *We are at all times aware of being part of a bigger family.*

The Word of God declares:

> But you [collectively] are a chosen people, a royal priesthood, a holy nation, a people belonging to God, that you [collectively] may declare the praises of him who called you out of darkness into his wonderful light. Once you were not a people, but now you are the people of God (1 Pet. 2:9,10, *NIV*).

Nowhere in this text is there any language dividing us into segments of people in order to accomplish God's purpose of declaring His glory in the earth. Instead it is clear from Scripture that our heavenly Father sees us all as His tiyospaye, extended family, and oyate kin, the people. The Church worldwide can learn from their Native brethren to see themselves more as parts of a greater whole.

The Traditional Male Role

Before the reservations, Native men of many tribes proved themselves through warring and hunting. Men were tested for bravery, courage and a willingness to risk their lives for the good of the community. As warriors they gained respect, self-worth, a sense of pride and, often, power, prestige and wealth. Warriors were the heroes, and many a warrior became a chief by distinguishing himself in battle.

Bravery was a foremost virtue for both men and women. Hunters and warriors were respected according to the number of times they had accomplished brave deeds. Among the Sioux and many Northern Plains tribes, the greatest honor in personal combat was called counting coup. To count coup was to touch the enemy and to escape without harm. War was often thought to be a wonderful game.

Native men took care of their families. Food, clothing and shelter were provided as a result of their prowess, skill and courage as hunters. Hunters were men of honor who enjoyed respect in the community and a strong sense of self-esteem and worth. Generosity was the sign of a true leader.

But with the advent of the reservation, Native men were no longer able to go to war and to provide for their families through hunting. So the disintegration of traditional male roles began in

Native cultures. (The loss of traditional male roles has infected almost all cultures today, to one degree or another.) For years fathers, grandfathers and uncles had interacted with and mentored the young men. However, when the tradional male roles were discontinued, the older men had nothing to pass on to the younger.

Some historians have said that the worth and character of a people may be judged by the actions of its soldiers in battle. In their own lost cause, Native warriors faced death courageously. Later, in the two World Wars they stood side by side with their White brothers and unflinchingly and calmly fought for the same causes as their forefathers: their families, the land they loved, freedom.

Though they fought on equal terms and with as much courage as their White comrades, the rewards for Native soldiers have not been equal. With the exception of Vietnam, White men came home knowing who they were and where they stood in social terms; but when the honor in war was done, Red men (and other minorities) had no identity or assigned virtue as part of American society.

The Role of Children

Traditionally, Native girls were under female supervision throughout their lives; boys were under female supervision until they were between six and eight years of age. Fathers then began schooling their sons. Teaching was done not just by the fathers but also by grandfathers, uncles, older cousins—the whole tribe took responsibility for the upbringing of children. And in Native culture *children participated in adult activities*; whereas in the Western culture, parents and teachers have historically interacted with their young by participating in children's activities.

Today Native grandparents still take a large and active role in raising children. Natives hold great respect and admiration for their elders, who are highly valued and considered to be the keepers of wisdom, traditional values, customs and knowledge.

Native children by and large are not "disciplined," however—at least not in the Anglo-evangelical sense of the word. One characteristic of child raising that has not changed much among most tribes is the almost complete freedom given to children. Love and affection are lavished upon the young, and they are allowed to run in an unruly and undisciplined manner.

No sacrifice is too great to make for a child. Native mothers have been known to sell their best and most valued possessions in order to raise money to send a child to school. For generations, Native children have been taught that respect and obedience are due their parents because of the sacrifices their parents make. Each child was taught that when he was weak and could not care for himself, the parents were strong; then, as the parents would grow weak with age, the child would grow strong and must care for them.

Today, because of the continuing disintegration of traditional family structures, children suffer the most. I once saw a billboard that read, "CHILDREN are the pieces of a broken marriage." This identifies poignantly the sad predicament of Native youth in "Indian country" today. Because there is such a high incidence of abuse, neglect, cultural deterioration and alcohol abuse in the home, Native youth live under tremendous pressures.

Bea Medicine, an Oglala Sioux woman, writes:

Nowhere in contemporary Oglala culture are the signs of social disorganization more apparent than in the institution of the family. There are greater and increasing role incompatibilities. The ability of the Dakota family to meet the stresses and strains of acculturation and adaptation has crippled, it would seem, the total framework of Dakota (Sioux) individuals.[4]

The present instability of the Native family can be traced to a number of factors. One significant cause was the misguided and arrogant policy of forced acculturation. Other factors include:

- impoverishment due to loss of an economic base;
- the decline of the role of the male;
- the taking over of family functions by government agencies; and
- the loss of traditional roles in the kinship system that defined behavior.

Some results of disruptions within the family structure are:

- loss of controls—the family is less able to control the actions of its members;
- the weakening of role models for the young;
- the loss of emotional security;
- increase in family strife;
- increased use and addiction to alcohol;
- juvenile delinquency and behavior problems;
- academic underachievement;
- hopelessness on the part of the old and young; and
- greater instances of child neglect and abuse.

OVERCOMING OUR DIFFERENCES

Is the Native-Anglo discord as big as it seems? Yes and no.

Many variables shape modern Natives' views and perceptions of Anglo people. A few of the determining factors and influences include:

- Were they raised in a traditional or non-traditional religious home?
- Are they full-blooded Natives or mixed blood, and were they raised speaking their Native language?
- Were their early years spent on the reservation or in an urban area?
- Do they have a formal education?

Native people in their environment don't generally appreciate White do-gooders, Christian or otherwise, coming in to help them. Osage Indians used to say, "If you see a White man coming toward you with a gleam in his eye to help you, run like crazy the other way!" As often as not, the reason for this reaction is that what motivates a person to help is a sense of either superiority or guilt. The motive is not necessarily to meet the needs of the Native but, rather, the need of the one coming to do some kind of conscience-salving relief work.

I spoke of attitudes earlier. I still find many Anglo Evangelicals who have condescending attitudes toward Native peoples. They are still trying to help "the poor Indian." They take up old clothes and hold canned-food drives and take these out to the reservations. Then the church members feel better that they have helped—better than the poor people they tried to help. The hidden side of this transaction often does more harm than good.

As we have seen, the flow of resources, services and ministry in Native and White Christian communities is typically a one-way flow. Thankfully, a growing number of White church leaders are recognizing their need to be equipped by or ministered to

by their Native brethren. But not enough have seen the light—
the eye doesn't yet realize that without the foot it can never really fully be the eye. I hope that someday the playing field will be
leveled and we will all work as equal partners to establish
Christ's kingdom here on earth.

Most Native people pick up on outsiders' attitudes right
away. It is important to understand what we think about others
of different ethnic backgrounds and why. Those with an interest
to help really should consider what they think and why before
venturing off to work among those of a different cultural background, whether overseas or across town.

One of the things we have learned through the centuries is
that humor is a great means of crossing cultural barriers.
Humor is a universal bridge that we all share and enjoy. I doubt
you'll find a people with a more pronounced sense of humor
than Native Americans. Regardless of negative circumstances
and disparaging conditions, we can still laugh and enjoy the
irony and humor of life. We will stop and laugh at a good story
(usually about ourselves) at the drop of a hat. As a matter of fact,
despite many centuries of oppression, injustice and struggle,
there is one thing that we as Native people have learned: When
the chips are down, the buffalo is empty.

CHAPTER FIVE

WHY SHOULD THE DEVIL HAVE ALL THE GOOD MUSIC?

I felt as though I had taken a step back in time to the days of Ghengis Khan and the Golden Horde. As I looked out over the Mongolian *ghers* (traditional round, felt-covered tents), the beauty of the rolling hills and roaming herds of horses, my mind wandered back to my history books where I had read how the ancestors of these simple herdsman had nearly conquered the world. Aside from some modern utensils, clothing and materials, the scene before me could have been set a thousand years ago. The people, especially the youth, swarmed all around us, wanting to hear what we Indians from America had to say.

During our visit to Mongolia, my Native companions and I were treated with great honor and respect as men of the First Nations. While there, we were privileged to witness an amazing event as dozens of young teenagers and preteens competed in a grueling 12-mile horse race across the countryside. The ground shook with a thunderous roar as these huge horses flew by us with often tiny-looking 9- to 14-year-old children on their backs.

On numerous occasions I was treated to a bowl of their customary social drink, *arik*, a fermented drink made from mare's milk. If you can imagine a drink of equal parts of champagne and buttermilk, you get some idea of the taste of arik. While visiting the gher of a Mongol horse trainer, we were offered a bowl of arik. But before offering me the drink, the man poured a bowl of arik and then unexpectedly tossed it into the air and said some words I didn't understand. I later learned that in Mongolia it is a common custom to offer a bowl of arik to the spirit of the mountain as an expression of thanksgiving.

Rick Leatherwood, my friend in Mongolia, explained to me that many Christian missionaries had told new believers they must stop throwing horse milk in the air now that they were Christians because it was an idolatrous practice. Their response to this traditional practice serves as a clear illustration of how well-meaning but misguided Christians and missionaries tend to interpret other peoples' cultural and religious practices through the filter of their own cultural preferences.

Rick had challenged the missionaries, asking them where in the Bible was found a prohibition against throwing horse milk. The problem was not in the throwing, they said, but in the idolatry of offering praise to another god. So Rick encouraged new Mongolian believers to continue to give a "heave offering" of their mare's milk as an expression of gratitude to the God of heaven and His Son, Jesus Christ. This is a classic example of how a cultural custom can be reinterpreted and redeemed from its former idolatrous usage and sanctified to express Christian faith, without disparaging Native culture.

CULTURAL PREFERENCES AND
BIBLICAL STANDARDS

It is most difficult for any of us to resist the temptation to attach a biblical value to our own cultural preferences or distinctives, as though no other culture could be as biblical or valuable as ours. Many Western missionaries over the past few centuries have couched the gospel in their own cultural distinctives—language, musical instruments, housing structures—as though these preferences were biblical or holy, often declaring outright that the cultural preferences of the indigenous peoples were in fact unbiblical or unholy. Because we are all so prone to be culturally egocentric, the temptation is to consider our worldview *the* biblical and correct one, shunning all others as unbiblical and wrong. Worse yet is our habit of judging cultural ways—songs, dances, rituals, etc.—to be sinful when there is no clear violation of Scripture.

Life for Native people is really no different from that of any others. We are born, we grow up and marry, we have children, we grow old, and we all die. It is the way of all things. King Solomon in the book of Ecclesiastes discussed the circular and cyclical movement of life through the ages:

Generations come and generations go, but the earth remains forever. The sun rises and the sun sets, and hurries back to where it rises. The wind blows to the south and turns to the north; round and round it goes, ever returning on its course. All streams flow into the sea, yet the sea is never full. To the place the streams come from, there they return again. . . . What has been will be again, what has been done will be done again; there is nothing new under the sun. Is there anything of which one can say, "Look! This is something new"? It was here already, long ago; it was here before our time.

Whatever is has already been, and what will be has been before; and God will call the past to account (Eccles. 1:4-7,9,10; 3:15, *NIV*).

CLASHING WORLDVIEWS

Different people groups have different ways of defining value, worth and beauty. Some cultures, for example, place a high value on aesthetics—how something looks, its appeal to the eye, the attractiveness of its outward appearance. Others value an object for its utilitarian function—its practical application or purpose. The following story illustrates these different valuations:

One day two boys, one Native and one Anglo, were playing catch with a baseball. It was a bad day for playing catch, because on this day each boy threw the ball through the front window of their respective houses, which happened to be next door to each other.

The next day the father of the Caucasian boy went down to the glass shop and purchased a new pane of glass. He came home and repaired his broken window beautifully. The Native father went into his garage and found some good clear plastic and duct tape and repaired his window, also beautifully.

Several weeks passed and the Anglo fellow wondered if the Native fellow was ever going to get around to fixing his broken window. Both men attended the same church, and the Anglo man soon worked up the courage to speak to his Native brother. When asked when he planned to get around to repairing his window, the Native man said, "It is fixed. It keeps the rain, wind, bugs and dirt out just fine."

The Anglo fellow went on complaining to his wife about the unsightly, embarrassing and ugly plastic on his neighbor's "unrepaired" window.

The Anglo brother's culture placed a high value on how things looked. The Native brother's culture valued the practicality of fixing the window so that it would accomplish its purpose.

Suppose God were to comment on this incident. When He looked at the repairs of the Anglo fellow, He might say something like, "Well done! What a beautiful repair job." Regarding the Native fellow's repair, would He then say, "My, not a very good-looking job"? Let me ask you a silly question. Do you believe God has a preference for glass or plastic windows? I doubt it. But the problem is that *we* do.

On this side of heaven, we have all kinds of cultural, national and personal preferences and biases. And we each want to believe that God looks, thinks and has the same preferences and viewpoints as we do. White Americans tend to think our Lord speaks English; is White like them with sandy-blond hair, blue eyes and a fair complexion; and lives in a mansion similar to the White House. African-Americans want to believe Jesus is Black. Among the Natives, we think He is a brown-skinned, dark-haired, dark-eyed member of the tribe of Judah. He even fluently speaks Navajo, Kiowa, Sioux, Apache and 250 other tribal languages from North America.

Our different perspectives become a problem when an Anglo brother says to his Native Christian neighbor, "The Bible teaches we are to be good stewards of things. It is the duty of Christians to keep our things clean, pretty and appealing. This pleases God." The Native brother thinks (but usually does not say), *I can't see where the Bible teaches that a washed, shiny car brings any more glory to God than a dusty one.*

When one cultural group exalts its cultural preferences as though they are—or ought to be—the biblical standard or norm for all others to follow, this is ethnocentrism.

WHY SHOULD THE DEVIL HAVE ALL THE GOOD MUSIC?

In the mid-1970s, a Christian rock musician named Larry Norman wrote a song titled "Why Should the Devil Have All the Good Music?" The lyrics spoke of the mainstream churches' rigid opposition to the early expressions of Christian rock music and to any attempt to introduce this style of worship into the Church. Rock music was labeled ungodly and thought to be of the devil. Larry Norman was asking why we should surrender God's good music—the cultural preference of Larry's generation—to the thievery and misuse of Satan.

If I were to blindfold you and take you to several ethnic churches and ask you to guess which ethnic group's church service you were attending, I believe this would turn out to be a fun and revealing experiment. You might quickly and correctly identify an African-American church, Hispanic church, Korean church and Latino church. But if I were to take you to a Native American church, 90 percent of the time you *would not know* based on the musical, linguistic or liturgical content that you were attending a Native church service. In almost no Indian churches would you ever hear a drum, rattle, flute or gourd used in Christian worship. Instead, you would hear songs from the same hymnbook most Anglo churches might use, accompanied by a piano, organ, guitars—all non-Native Western musical forms and styles. Many visitors to Indian churches identify a Southern gospel sound as an Indian musical style or form. The reason is the same ethnocentric cultural bias against the music of indigenous peoples.

I once read that the only style of music acceptable for Christian worship was European classical music. The author, Lowell Hurst, wrote, "Music of the world appeals to the flesh and the old nature," listing African drumming, jazz, country and western, rock and roll, soul, swing and blues as worldly music. Presumably Native American drums, musical forms, flutes, rattles and sounds would also fit his description of "Satan's sinister seduction . . . an attempt to erode the solid Rock on which we stand." Mr. Hurst went on to say that the "traditional music of the Church"—hymns, Reformation-era music, anthems and gospel songs—appeals to our spirits and our new nature. Ironically, Mr. Hurst wrote of church music, "Music is being substituted for the solid meat of Luther, Wesley, Watts and Sankey"—all great writers of early hymns.[1]

Yet such well-known hymn writers as Charles Wesley are known to have taken popular tavern songs of their day and simply changed the words of these worldly, hedonistic songs to make them Christian. Wesley sensed that a people's culture is the medium of God's revelation to them. He sensed that when the cultural form of ministry fits the people, they have a better chance of responding than if the cultural forms are alien to them.

Anyone who feels that Native American music (or the music of any other culture) is unacceptable in the Christian realm could easily say, "I disagree with you and cannot participate personally. But if you believe you have God's favor and grace, go for it. I'll not judge and condemn you." Wouldn't that be more loving than to label a particular culture's music as satanic?

A Native brother, and close friend, once told me that he and another brother had conducted some Sunday services on a reservation in the Midwest. One led worship with a guitar, while the other accompanied him with a traditional hand drum. They had a great service, with people making decisions for Christ and commitments to serve the Lord.

As they were eating together afterward, a member of the church asked my friend and his partner if they had noticed the glow surrounding them while they were leading worship. Another member at the table said he had seen the same thing. My friend and his companion hadn't noticed anything unusual but concluded it must have been the presence of the Lord.

Around the world, traditional

musical forms are being

adopted by the Church as

legitimate expressions of

biblical faith and worship.

A short time later my friend related this incident to some other Native leaders. When he had finished, one of the older men present, a man who had been a believer for more than 40 years, stated that the glow must have been a demonic manifestation. His reasoning was that God cannot bless our Native drums, so it could not have been the Spirit of the Lord but was something from the devil.

Remarkably, this is not an extreme opinion in the Native church. As a matter of fact, for the past 50 years a similar opinion has been held by most Native believers and leaders.

Yet we see that around the world there is a great resurgence of traditional musical forms being adapted for church use as legitimate expressions of biblical faith and worship. Various worship leaders and songwriters in the Body of Christ are now using Native instruments and styles in their worship music.

SAVED THROUGH THE WITNESS
OF THE AFRICAN DRUM

After I had finished speaking at a conference in Portage LaPrairie, Ontario, Canada, a gentleman came up to me and related a very wonderful and enlightening story. I asked him to write it down and send it to me. Ian Ritchie, Ph.D., is an assistant professor of religion and culture at Concord College and was a missionary in Africa for a number of years. He wrote:

Richard, I affirm you strongly in your vision of how North American Native Christians have a unique opportunity worldwide right now to share the gospel. My prayers are with you in your endeavors! It would be just wonderful if you could take a team to one of the Arab countries or an African country where Islam is influential.

The following story, which I asked Dr. Ritchie to send to me, is a powerful example of how deep areas of people's faith and belief can be influenced by cultural expressions, particularly tribal music. Dr. Ritchie told me that often the African drum was banned by missionaries on the grounds that it was demonic. "But in the African Independent Churches [often now called African-Initiated Churches] drums were and are used in the worship of God since their early days in the beginning of this century," wrote Dr. Ritchie. "By the 1970s, even the indigenous daughter churches of the missionaries were accepting the use of the drum in worship services in church."

Here is Ian's story:

I heard the story when I lived in Nigeria between 1980 and 1985 about a man who converted to Christianity largely as a result of the Christian use of drums. The man had been born into a home where the African Traditional Religion was practiced. But at a fairly early age his parents converted to Islam and so he went to the mosque after that.

At the mosque, people never were allowed to use drums in the worship of Allah, because it is believed in the Islamic faith that each individual drum contains its own "jinn," or spirit. Thus, Muslims may use drums in music away from the Mosque, but at the Mosque during worship drums may not be used in the worship of Allah.

Well, one day the man was walking down a path, which took him by a local Christian church. Inside the people were singing and praising God, and they were playing African drums in their worship of God. They were singing a melody which he had remembered from his childhood in the African Traditional Religion, and which he had always loved. He had always wanted to sing that song again, but since his family had become Muslim they had never sung it.

The man was so intrigued by the sound of the song that he stopped; and then he entered into the church, something that Muslims don't often do. The song that had so fascinated him had Christian words set to the melody he had known from his childhood. The man soon became a Christian. He was impressed that the Christians believed that the power of God is stronger than the power of the jinn, and so Jesus can drive out the evil spirits from any drum. The question boiled down to this: Who is stronger, Jesus or Satan? Christians believe that Jesus is stronger; that he is able to overcome all evil. Now, Muslims also believe that Allah is stronger than the devil, at least in theory. But in the case of this church and this man, it became evident that it was really the

Christians who demonstrated by their actions that it is God who is stronger.

The man thought, *If we say that God is stronger than Satan, then why wouldn't it be possible for God to drive out the jinn from the drum?* It seemed to him that it was really the Christians, after all, who not only believed it, but put it into practice. And the question of practice is very important, particularly for Muslims. It has long been observed that Muslims are, of all the people groups of the world, the most resistant to the gospel of Jesus Christ. But there are many Muslims, especially in Africa, who might be open to a culturally appropriate form of worship and praise to God.

What a great example of how the Holy Spirit can speak to the heart of the nonbeliever through our Native music and instruments! God is not offended or afraid of our Native beats, rhythms, syncopation, minor chords, musical emotion, sounds or instruments. Some in the Body of Christ have propagated an unfounded fear of tribal music that is based entirely on ethnocentric conjecture and cultural arrogance.

CAN GOD USE OUR POWWOW DRUM?

Here is a heartwarming story of the Holy Spirit using our North American powwow drum. My wife, Katherine, wrote this report about how God used the playing of the drum in a wonderful way in the life of one of our sons:

It was a fun, uplifting time that was interrupted by a nudge from our 19-year-old son, Andrew, who pointed to his 11-year-old brother, Daniel. He was in the back of the room, obviously upset and crying. I went to him to see what was the matter.

We were in Fairbanks, Alaska, as part of an outreach at the World Eskimo Indian Olympics, hosted by Doug Yates and his ministry, Young Warriors. On this particular evening we were concluding our team orientation with a time of praise and worship. We were led in worship by a local group of young people from Fairbanks, along with some of our team members. The musicians with all their instruments were on one end of the room, and in the center of the floor was a large powwow-style drum. Four chairs were pulled up around it, and as worship began, so did the unified drumming of the four men around the large drum. We were singing and worshiping, and after a time those who had begun on the large drum got up and invited others in the room to take a turn. More drumsticks were produced, chairs were added and worship ebbed and flowed all around us. I watched as first Richard drummed, who then invited Andrew, who in turn handed the drumstick to me. After a time I gave my drumstick back to Richard, who went and got our youngest son, Daniel. It was very moving to watch our sons playing with such enjoyment and pride. But now here was Daniel crying.

He tried to assure me that nothing had happened to him, and as I pressed him to find out what was bothering him, he said he didn't actually know. We then stepped outside, followed by Richard. Daniel kept repeating that he wasn't hurt, that he hadn't done anything wrong, and no one had said anything harsh to him. Really puzzled by his tears and inability to say what was bothering him, we were prompted to go to our van for more privacy. We gently probed, trying to help Daniel verbalize what had happened. When for the third time he could only say, "I don't know what's wrong," a light began to dawn within us. We explained to him that sometimes, in times of worship to Jesus, His spirit touches our hearts, and sometimes we cry. That got Daniel's attention, and in the course of the next 15 minutes or so, we were able to share with Daniel about God's great love for him. We then had the very great privilege of listening as our son opened his life to Jesus. We watched as he stepped from one kingdom into another.

As Daniel now had a little perspective on what had been happening to him, he was able to relate when it had all started. He said, "You know, I really felt like crying when I was playing the big drum." In the specialness of the moment we were quite struck with when and how God touched our son. Richard told Daniel that the vision for playing the drum was to honor Jesus, and before the drummers began playing the drum, they had prayed over the drum that the Holy Spirit would minister to people and use the drum music to draw people closer to Jesus. Daniel innocently replied, "Well, I guess it worked, didn't it?"

WHAT IS CHRISTIAN MUSIC?

When a person believes that Christian music is Christian by virtue of a particular kind of sound, style or structure, he or she commits a grievous mistake by trying to assign a moral and ethical value to an art form, to mere handiwork. Harold M. Best wrote in his book *Music Through the Eyes of Faith*:

> This kind of thinking is in "idol territory," and whenever it appears, it confuses and divides. Theologically it is in fact contrary to every biblical and creational doctrine and has nearly thoroughly stripped the Native church of all of its indigenous music.
>
> Musical pentecost is not one music pitted against another. It is a sharing, a commingling, a co-celebration, a co-usage among many tongues. Artistic pentecost is community. It unifies. It brings the bagpipes of Scotland in union with the balalaikas of Russia; it tunes the nose flute of Papua New Guinea to the marimbas of Guatemala and joins the Jesus rap of the inner city to intercourse with the gamelan of Bali.
>
> If we genuinely love *ourselves*, culturally and ethnically, we will naturally love the ways of others. To love our own musical ways brings us the resilience, assurance, and freedom to look lovingly into the musical ways of others and even to be nurtured by them. This is simply the Golden Rule stated musically: If and as I truly love my immediate musical world, I will be able to understand the love of others for their ways.
>
> Music has no interior beacon that guarantees permanent meaning. Unlike truth . . . music can shift in meaning from place to place and time to time. Of all the art forms music is inherently most flexible. Music, as music, is completely relative.[2]

By now it should be obvious to all of us that no one culture can say it all. I am seeing believers of all traditions who appreciate the sounds of worship endeavoring to join the creative ways of other cultures, if for no other reason than to catch a greater vision of the fullness of God!

As I look and observe the Spirit of God unite the hearts of God's people in many cultural expressions of praise and worship, I see not only a holy communion but tremendous liberty and joy. We catch a glimpse of heavenly worship as many tongues become the common song, and the Body of Christ, in all of its parts, freely joins in singing, "Worthy is the Lamb." How awesome it is to see and hear the war drums of the First Nations people being used for the glory of almighty God!

I have written worship songs to Jesus Christ using the traditional style, structures, language and sound of the Lakota people. I have sung these songs, while playing my traditional hand drum, in churches and conferences across North America, almost always with the same results: People are deeply touched, spiritually edified and often moved to tears. On several occasions, including a national Promise Keepers conference, the audience has risen to its feet in a prolonged standing ovation as I concluded my message with a Native prayer/drum song. My old "pagan" prayer song is being used for the glory of God. Because music is flexible and able to be reinterpreted, old Indian music styles can become sacred, or Christian, not by reason of form but through context and meaning.

As has been true throughout Church history, art in its many forms—whether a tavern song or a pagan symbol—can be gradually adapted to sacred use. Rock-and-roll music is one of the most obvious examples, in that its eventual acceptance by the Church shows how people consider music to be organically linked to the activities of everyday life and, therefore, find it inseparable from their belief systems. When these ties between belief and everyday life are misunderstood, the results are false assumptions about the nature of God's handiwork. In the Early

Church, Paul warned new believers against continuing in certain practices until they were spiritually strong enough to see the artificiality of its tie to a former belief. Once they were able to do this, they could then clearly see meat for what is—grub—and the idol for what it truly is—powerless sticks and stones (see Rom. 14:1-23; 1 Cor. 8:1-13). And what is true of meat and idols is equally true of music.

MIXING CHRISTIAN FAITH WITH FALSE RELIGIONS: THE DANGERS OF SYNCRETISM

People have some honest and legitimate questions about some of our Native traditions. I have been cautioned by some Christians to be careful not to introduce "Indian spirits" or to compromise God's Word in the process of using First Nations cultural expressions in worship.

Because many believers have a strong, inherent distrust of indigenous cultures and cultural expressions, the issue of *syncretism* is of great concern for many Christian people and for Native leaders. Rev. Adrian Jacobs offers this definition of syncretism:

> Syncretism is the attempted reconciliation or union of different or opposing principles or practices or parties, as in philosophy or religion. It is the attempted union of principles of parties irreconcilably at variance with each other, especially the doctrines of certain religionists.[3]

As it relates to the Native work, syncretism is an attempt to marry biblical Christian faith to incompatible or opposing Native religious beliefs. The syncretist sees the similarities between

Christianity and the Indian way and, without qualification, assumes they are the same and puts them together.

One distinct form of syncretism is referred to as Christopagan Syncretism or christopaganism. This sort of syncretism has to do with a people adopting foreign forms but interpreting them largely in local ways—there is a connection of new forms with old meanings, ideas and practices. For example, many of the sacraments of the Roman Catholic Church were interpreted by the local tribal peoples in Latin America as being the same as their own religious rituals. So they simply renamed their sun god God the Father or called their volcano spirit the Holy Spirit. Many so-called Christian rituals were viewed by the indigenous peoples as magical ceremonies, so local healers continued practicing their black magic alongside the Christian "magic." This often resulted in a combination of animal sacrifices and/or the use of fetishes with Catholic sacraments, creating a very superstitious concoction.

The American Indian Church would be another example of this. In their services they use the Bible and sing Christian songs. Yet the one thing that sets them apart is their prescribed use of the hallucinogenic drug found in peyote as part of their liturgy. The peyote is intended to increase one's receptiveness to God, therefore resulting in the participant's being more holy and closer to God. This is an attempt to form one new religion out of two old belief systems—a religion that is neither Christian nor traditionally Native. This is syncretism.

I have given a great deal of prayer and study to this issue. In light of numerous academic definitions, I would like to suggest that syncretism is much more than an application, misuse or practice of a cultural form, whether it be music, language, dance, custom, social practice, ceremony, art, etc. Based on my considerable biblical research and dialogue with those in the Christian academic community, I submit the following definitions:

1. Syncretism is a belief or practice, whether in an Anglo church on Sunday morning or in a Native ceremony, that attempts to replace or distort the historical doctrines of justification, righteousness, atonement, holiness, redemption, sanctification, salvation, etc.
2. Syncretism is anything that tries to replace, augment or add to the long-standing doctrines of historical Christianity.
3. Syncretism is any belief or practice that says Christ's work is not enough.

To best understand the issue of syncretism we need to consider its theological and doctrinal implications rather than to solely observe sociocultural forms and practices. By "sociocultural" I simply mean a position or belief based on a person's subjective personal life experiences—both social and cultural. It seems that many people today confuse the two until what we end up with in the Native work is confusion and division over some cultural practices.

Let me explain this further using the story a Native woman told me. A Christian Native friend of hers had been experiencing some spiritual warfare and, while praying, felt the Holy Spirit revealed to her that the entry point of this spiritual attack was the bracelet she was wearing. The bracelet was designed with some traditional tribal decoration. The woman felt impressed to get rid of it, so she and two friends went to a nearby river and she tossed the bracelet into the water. To their shock and surprise, the bracelet flew back out of the water and landed at her feet on the shore. The friends prayed again—with a little more fervor this time—and the woman threw the bracelet in again. This time it disappeared into the water. Afterward the lady was fine and the warfare ceased.

Do I believe this sort of thing happens? Absolutely! Do I believe that demonic spirits can somehow attach themselves to physical objects? I have no doubt.

But now let me explain how this personal experience can become a sociocultural standard. Did the Holy Spirit reveal to the woman to get rid of her Native bracelet? I have no reason to question that He did. Does the Bible prohibit the wearing of bracelets as jewelry? No. What about tribal or Native jewelry? No. But because the Lord moved in this woman's life in the particular way that He did regarding her bracelet, the woman and her two friends concluded that *all* Native bracelets with *similar* tribal designs are demonized and should not be worn by Christians. Because of their personal, subjective experience, they came to believe that wearing such things is syncretistic and compromising of God's standards of holiness.

The fact is that not all Native bracelets with similar tribal designs are evil. Let's say a Christian silversmith fashions a beautiful bracelet with traditional tribal designs that reflect his or her love of Christ and His creation. The bracelet has a distinct, God-honoring meaning, but its design strongly resembles that of the bracelet thrown into the river. A sociocultural definition of syncretism says that because the bracelets are *similar*, they are identical; thus the new bracelet cannot be worn. This attitude is based purely on subjective, personal experience, not on revealed biblical doctrine and clear theology. This is an experience-based position—man-made rather than biblical.

Regarding the essential beliefs of orthodox evangelical Christianity, syncretism is any belief or practice that tries to do for a person what only Christ has done on the cross and continues, through salvation, to do today. *Theologically and doctrinally, I am adamantly opposed to syncretism in any form that in any way encroaches on the authority of God's Word and the work of the Cross.*

Though I agree we must be careful not to become a stumbling block to new believers or weak and undisciplined believers in how we use our liberty in Christ (see Rom. 14:1-23), we must be willing to employ whatever means necessary to see our Native people redeemed in Christ and saved from an eternity of separation from God:

> I have become all things to all men, that I might by all means save some (1 Cor. 9:22).

Are we willing to become culturally relevant to reach the Native tribes for the sake of the gospel?

Bill Hybels, founder and senior pastor of the 17,000-member Willow Creek Community Church near Chicago, describes how committed we need to be to win the lost. He says, "We will do anything just short of sin to win lost people to Jesus Christ." Is he saying we should intentionally see how close we can get to sinning without sinning? Obviously not! Yet how far are we willing to go to reach lost people, in particular, Native people?

God went so far as to sacrifice His Son. Jesus went so far as to identify completely with His Hebrew people and their culture. He went to their weddings; took part in their feasts; spent time visiting in the homes of drunkards, prostitutes and criminals; used the cultural forms and practices of the Hebrews to communicate cross-culturally the deep truths of the Father so people could understand them; worshiped in their temples; wept with them at funerals and, finally, took the sin of the people upon Himself and paid the ultimate price with His life.

Are we willing to become weak for those who are weak, under the law for those in bondage, traditional for the traditionalist and culturally relevant like the apostle Paul to reach the Native tribes for the sake of the gospel? Can we use our liberty in Christ to go to the places where lost people go? I think perhaps we have, at times, been more afraid of becoming a stumbling block to the 3 percent (of Natives who have accepted Christ) than we are determined to take the gospel to the 97 percent.

CULTURAL SYNCRETISM

Cultural syncretism is a fact of life. America is the epitome of cultural syncretism. Our nation is called the melting pot of the world because its culture is a blend or mixture of the cultural expression of the peoples of the earth. Nearly the entire population of North America is made up of immigrants from other countries, and its culture is a unique blend of the languages, music, dance, arts, economic systems, political structures, technology and sciences of its citizens. Culturally speaking, the United States of America is a syncretistic nation.

In the history of our tribes, Natives often exchanged songs, ceremonies, values, weapons and artifacts that were unique to a geographic region. When horses were introduced to the plains by the Spanish, the cultures and lifestyles of the first tribes to acquire them were radically altered. Sedentary societies of farmers/gatherers soon became known as nomadic warriors and hunters. The horse was far more than a beast of burden among the Natives; it represented a way of life. In terms of its effect on the Plains tribes, the horse was technology and industry at its finest. When introduced through trade to other tribes, horses became an immeasurable catalyst of cultural transformation. This is another example of cultural syncretism, a mixing or blending of two cultural lifestyles to become something previously unknown.

Incense and Prayer

In the book of Revelation there are two references to incense being the prayers of the saints:

> The twenty-four elders fell down before the Lamb, each having a harp, and golden bowls full of incense, which are the prayers of the saints (Rev. 5:8).

> Then another angel, having a golden censer, came and stood at the altar. He was given much incense, that he should offer it with the prayers of all the saints upon the golden altar which was before the throne. And the smoke of the incense, with the prayers of the saints, ascended before God from the angel's hand (Rev. 8:3,4).

Suppose Christians, purely for its ascetic value, enjoy the fragrant aroma of burning frankincense. Now suppose they find it personally meaningful to occasionally burn the incense during their prayer time because it reminds them that, symbolically and literally, their prayers are like incense that rises up to the very throne of God. The smell and smoke also remind them symbolically that, through faith in Jesus Christ, God hears and answers prayer. Can you see anything wrong with this picture?

Now change the scenario and imagine Native believers enjoying the fragrant aroma of burning sage, sweet grass or cedar—in effect, incense. Imagine that these Native believers are also symbolically reminded by the sight of the ascending smoke and aroma of the burning cedar bark that their prayers are literally ascending upward to the very presence of God. The combination of smoke and smell is a symbol or picture to them of the prayers of the saints spoken of in the Bible. Can you see anything wrong with *this* picture?

For many First Nations believers, the above example would clearly be seen as syncretism. In many Plains tribal traditions, their purification and prayer ceremonies often involve smudging: A brand of sage, sweet grass or cedar is lit with fire and allowed to smolder and smoke. Then a person fans the smoke over himself or others or into the air with his hand or a feather. It is believed that the smoke does two things: (1) It has the power to cleanse and purify; and (2) it takes our prayers and carries them up into heaven to the Creator.

Now, armed with this new information, do you see anything wrong with the picture of the believer praying and worshiping while enjoying the fragrance of cedar smoke?

Traditional Native Drums

Imagine 120 drums all being played in worship to Jesus Christ. God has given my friend Lynda Prince a vision to see our Native music used in prophetic worship among the nations. A group of believers have handcrafted 120 drums with one large center drum having four different designs. The designs are taken from chapter 4 of Revelation:

> Surrounding the throne were twenty-four other thrones, and seated on them were twenty-four elders. . . . In the center, around the throne, were four living creatures, and they were covered with eyes, in front and in back.

The first living creature was like a lion, the second was like an ox, the third had a face like a man, the fourth was like a flying eagle. Each of the four living creatures had six wings and was covered with eyes all around, even under his wings. Day and night they never stop saying: "Holy, holy, holy is the Lord God Almighty, who was, and is, and is to come" (Rev. 4:4,6-8, *NIV*).

Thirty drums bear the design of an ox, 30 have an eagle feather, 30 a lion and 30 a face like a man. This team has carried out a very unique ministry across the land through drumming, music and dance; and their drums have been used to point people to Jesus through worship. These Natives led the worship procession at the final Feast of Tabernacles of the millennium in Jerusalem last year. At a worship conference I convened in Kansas City, the Many Nations One Voice Conference, several dozen Native dancers and 120 drums joined with Kevin Prosch for a wonderful time of praise and worship, resulting in numerous testimonies of people being set free from fear and bondages and released into newfound freedom.

All across Turtle Island (North America), a new sound is beginning to be heard in the Church. Praise and worship have always been a hallmark of spiritual renewal and revival in the earth, and I believe the Church is in for great blessings from the throne of God as this new sound of worship from First Nations people—the drum—is heard in the land.

Feathers

Each time one of my boys turns 13, we have a special gathering of friends and family to honor him. We prepare a meal for everyone, and I ask several men and women who have special areas of skill or success to say a few words of encouragement and challenge to my son from their area of strength. We give the boy his first leather-bound Bible with his name on it and a plaque inscribed with Isaiah 40:30,31 (*NIV*):

> Even youths grow tired and weary, and young men stumble and fall; but those who hope in the LORD will renew their strength. They will soar on wings like eagles; they will run and not grow weary, they will walk and not be faint.

Attached to the plaque is a beautiful and finely beaded eagle feather. The eagle feather is a visual and symbolic reminder of the biblical realities of youth and of putting his hope and faith in God. Even from a distance, when my sons can't read the text of Scripture inscribed on the plaque, the feather reminds them of the reality and truth of God's Word—that if they put their faith in Jesus Christ, they can soar like eagles in the midst of life's temptations and difficulties.

Christian Forms and Symbols

Christianity is loaded with forms, meanings and functions. There is nothing "Christian" in the origin of the cross. The cross was around a long time before the birth of Christ and was universally considered under Roman rule to be a symbol of human torture, suffering and death. Yet the shape of a cross (a symbol or form) has come to be forever identified with Christianity. Crowns, doves, fish shapes, steeples, pews and olive oil are other forms/symbols that have meaning to Christians and that fulfill a function. The forms themselves can mean something totally different to non-Christians. Turn the cross upside down, and it takes on a whole different meaning for a Satanist. Take the olive (anointing) oil into the kitchen, and it takes on a different function.

Why then are the traditional and ceremonial symbols and forms of Native Americans considered evil, unbiblical and unfit for use in a Christian context? I do not deny the spiritual warfare dynamic in many of these issues. I know there are times when some items that have been dedicated to the worship of idols or used in spiritistic practices should be discarded. I believe there are times when demonic strongholds must first be broken and the authority of Christ established in the use of some items, Native American or otherwise. But this should not be a blanket, across-the-board approach to all Native American symbols or forms.

Oftentimes it is we as Native leaders who must be careful not to allow biblical ignorance to lead to an unfounded fear of syncretism among ourselves. We must counsel, pray and dialogue to prevent fear of syncretism from becoming an emotionally defined standard for a type of modern-day inquisition, used to root and burn out of Native Christians any tie to our culture and traditions and, in the process, mislabeling faith in Christ as "the White man's religion" and leaving many Native people without hope for salvation.

The effectiveness of our prayers and intercession can be enhanced immeasurably by better awareness of history. I hope after reading this book you will be encouraged in your prayers for Native people and their role in God's intended purposes for our nation and our planet.

There are a growing number of ministries that are making efforts to genuinely come alongside and partner with their Native brethren. If this increases and becomes more effective, it will open many doors for the gospel at last to penetrate Native culture in a significant way. Our hope is that the 97 percent of Native people who don't yet know Christ will find new life in Him.

Native people have much to contribute to the life and the growth of the Body of Christ. As the host people of the land, our cultural distinctives can add a rich and valuable perspective to the approach and practice of spreading God's Word among non-Native believers. I conclude that we are in an epoch, a predetermined period of time, when the Church is ripe for the emergence of Native expressions of Christ and of His kingdom in North America and around the world.

"STEAL MY RAGE"
BY ROSE

You are listening but can you hear?
to hear involves the heart . . .
a lot of white people tell me that they too
have suffered in poverty
I believe them.
But I don't believe
they were beat up,
shut up, taunted or spit on for being white.
I have overcome the poverty
it's my self-esteem
that I am still
trying
to reclaim.[4]

CHAPTER SIX

CHIEF SPOKANE GARRY: APOSTLE IN HIS DAY

When my friend John drove me to the cemetery and we walked to the large stone that marked the burial site of Chief Spokane Garry in Spokane, Washington, I felt such incredible sadness and awe that I wept. On a later visit I went to Chief Garry's homestead, which had been stolen from him, and then drove through the small, wooded canyon where he lived his final days—rejected, broken, destitute, but still with a great love for Jesus in his heart. I believe the Church today needs to be introduced to Chief Garry.

In spite of his spiritual leadership and obvious commitment to Christ, the story of Chief Spokane Garry is one of the most revealing and heartbreaking episodes in the history of missions among the Native people. Many peoples and ethnic groups have their heroes and heroines of the faith: Dr. Martin Luther King, Jr., Watchman Nee, John Huss, John Wesley, Corrie ten Boom, Mother Theresa, Saint Patrick and many others. Chief Garry should be listed alongside these great men and women of faith, yet few people have ever heard of this Native American spiritual leader and man of God.

When I first became a Christian, I read and was greatly inspired by the stories of many great missionaries and leaders. Hudson Taylor, Jonathon Goforth, C. T. Studd and William Carey are all heroes for me. As I have come to know more about him, I believe Chief Garry can become an inspiration for Native Americans as Dr. King has been for the African-American community.

What follows is a brief glimpse into the life of Chief Garry, a man who at times struggled to adjust to the new ways—and evils— that the White man brought. Garry was a tribal leader, husband, father and advocate for justice and Christian values. He was not perfect; he had his failures and shortcomings. Yet one could clearly see he was a man committed to the Word of God and the Lordship of Jesus Christ. He lived and died as a follower of the Jesus Way.

GOD WAS ALREADY HERE

Throughout the history of missions, the Church has found that God was preparing people groups for the coming of the Messiah long before the first missionaries entered their lands. Here in North America, the God of the Bible—the God of Abraham, Isaac and Jacob—had been at work among the tribes of this land eons before the first European arrived.

> What may be known about God is plain to them, because God has made it plain to them. For since the creation of the world God's invisible qualities—his eternal power and divine nature—have been clearly seen,

being understood from what has been made, so that
men are without excuse (Rom. 1:19,20, *NIV*).

The witness of God—the natural revelation of creation—was so
strong on this continent that no tribal person could ever say as
an excuse, "We never knew of You."

Such is the case with the First Nations people who occupied
the Plateau area of western Montana, Wyoming, Idaho, eastern
Washington and Oregon. God had prepared the way for Chief
Spokane Garry, like the apostle Paul, to become God's chosen
servant and special messenger among his people.

CIRCLING RAVEN

In 1782, the first virgin-soil epidemic swept across the
American continent—an epidemic of smallpox. During this
mysterious sickness Circling Raven, a shaman of the Sin-ho-
man-naish (the Middle Spokanes) attempted to minister healing to his people who lived just west of present-day Spokane.
His shamanistic practices failed to heal them, however. A great
number of the villagers perished, and he, too, lost his son to the
disease.

Circling Raven suffered a crisis of faith. Disillusioned and
angry, he asked his brother, "If the righteous die while evil men
live, why should we continue to follow our laws? Let us live like
the animals."

But his brother persuaded the shaman to maintain his faith,
for a while longer, in their moral law and in the god they called
Quilent-sat-men, "He Made Us." He also persuaded Circling Raven
to go to the top of Mount Spokane for four days of prayer and
fasting.

At the conclusion of his fast, according to Spokane tradition, Circling Raven received a vision of men of white skin wearing strange clothes and bearing in their hands leaves bound together. He was told to counsel his people to prepare for these *chipixa*, "white-skinned ones," and to pay attention to the teaching that came from the leaves bound together.

SHINING SHIRT

Sometime during the eighteenth century, a Kalispel shaman and chief had delivered a similar message among the eastern Salish. According to ethnologist Harry Holbert Turney-High, the great cultural hero Shining Shirt prophesied that white people would come from the East one day.

According to legend, Shining Shirt was both a chief and a shaman. After Shining Shirt was grown and in charge of his people, a Power made a great revelation known to him. The Power said that there were a Good One and an Evil One of which the Indian knew but little so far. Yet the time would come when men with fair skins dressed in long black skirts would come and teach them the truth. These Indians had never heard of a white man at that early date.

The Black Robes would change the lives of the people in ways of which they had not dreamed. The Power then gave Shining Shirt a talisman of great strength: a piece of metal inscribed with a cross.

Shining Shirt forthwith assembled a council and preached and legislated according to the revelation. In the past, when a man married the elder sister of a family, all the younger ones automatically became his wives. Shining Shirt said the Power considered this a grievous error; therefore, all men must cleave solely to the elder sister and put the others away. He made himself an example by promptly divorcing the younger of his sister-wives.

Shining Shirt told the council that there is a God. His true name was not revealed, but He was called *Amotkan*, "He Who Lives on Most High." Shining Shirt said it was the people's duty to pray to Him, especially the chief who must do this every morning and particularly at the Midsummer Festival. Amotkan in some way had made the world and all the people, and to him all those who live good lives must return.

Shining Shirt then taught them that the Black Robes would give them a new moral law that they should obey. Again, these strange white men would teach them many things about making a living, of which they were then ignorant but which they must try to understand and perform as they were taught. Soon after their arrival, all wars would cease. Very soon after the appearance of the religious teachers, other men with white skins would come and simply overrun the country. They would make slaves of all the people, but they should not be resisted. This would only bring needless bloodshed.

Now the people trusted Shining Shirt and received his teaching. Even today they are convinced that he was given his power to accomplish an inevitable, divine purpose.

THE ARRIVAL OF THE FIRST WHITE MEN

In 1809 David Thompson, a Christian explorer and cartographer, led his fur brigades into the Columbia Plateau and established British fur-trading posts—two near the Kalispels and Flatheads and one among the Middle Spokanes. By 1825, interest in the chipixas' spiritual insights had grown to a fever pitch among the Plateau tribes.

On his first trip though the area in 1824-1825, George Simpson, governor of the northern department of the Hudson's

Bay Company, was accosted by a dozen chiefs requesting teachers to come among them and teach their people from the book they had seen at company posts. Simpson knew nothing of the prophecies that had fueled these requests.

While other tribes on the continent seem to have been interested mostly in the material benefits of White culture, Plateau tribes, by most accounts, were different. They wanted to know what the White people knew of the "Master of Life." Both Simpson and Alexander Ross of the Hudson's Bay Company were explicit about this unique characteristic of the Plateau tribes.[1]

SPOKANE GARRY IS BORN

Spokane Garry was born circa 1810. His father was Illim-Spokanee, the head chief of the Sin-ho-man-naish Indians. He was called Spokane, after the name of his tribe, and Garry, for one of the directors of the Hudson's Bay Company.

In 1825, with the permission and support of tribal leaders, George Simpson took two Indian boys in their early teens from the Middle Spokane and Lower Kootenay chiefs for the purpose of educating them at a Mission School at Red River, the site of present-day Winnipeg, Manitoba, Canada. The school was run by missionaries of the Church Missionary Society of the Church of England. The boys chosen were Kootenai Pelly and Spokane Garry.

When first presented with the idea, the tribal chiefs were indignant, asking if they were looked upon as dogs that were willing to give up their children to strange people and to send them somewhere they had never been. But when it was explained to them that they would be sent to a minister of religion to learn how to serve God, Chief Illim-Spokanee thoughtfully replied, "He might have hundreds of children in an hour's time." The chief then selected the sons of the two most powerful chiefs in that part of the country.[2]

The boys were brought before the White men. Chief Illim-Spokanee said, "You see, we have given you our children—not our servants or our slaves, but our own. We have given you our hearts—our children are our hearts—but bring them back again before they become White men. We wish to see them once more as Indians, and after that you can make them White men if you like. But let them not get sick or die. If they get sick, we get sick; if they die, we shall die. Take them, they are yours." So in 1825 Spokane Garry and Kootenai Pelly set out with the party of traders.[3]

GARRY GOES TO SCHOOL

Garry spent four years at the mission school, where he learned English, studied and memorized passages from the Bible and developed a life of prayer and worship. He used the Anglican Book of Common Prayer, memorized the catechism and learned the hymns and canticles of daily and Sunday worship services. Garry and Pelly became firm believers in peace between Indians and Whites, a belief that prevailed throughout Garry's life.

Garry and Pelly returned to Fort Colville in the summer of 1829. According to one author, after they returned to the fort, vast crowds gathered from hundreds of miles around to hear what these two young men might have to say about the Master of Life.

Garry was the first to teach God's Word among the Spokanes when he returned from Red River. He read to them from the Bible and taught the young and old from his prayer book. He showed the Indians the pictures and told them what was in the book. First Nations people came from the Colville, Nez Perce and Okanogan tribes to hear him.

Garry and Pelly made a tremendous impression on their own and neighboring tribes as they preached the Word of God. Their acceptance was phenomenal. Anthropologist Leslie Spier, who has studied the religious life of the Indians of this region, noted a remarkable spread of Christian practices among the tribes of this area and determined that the revival must have spread from the Spokane country about 1830 or a little later.

In 1832 the Rev. David T. Jones wrote to the Church Missionary Society in London that "the Indians on the upper part of the Columbia paid utmost attention to the information conveyed to them through the boys, Garry and Pelly, and readily received whatever instructions or doctrines they thought proper to inculcate . . . and ever since they assemble to keep the Sabbath in the ways the boys directed."[4]

That the Christian teachings of Garry and Pelly were readily accepted is further substantiated by one of the early Jesuit priests, Father P. Joset, who labored among these tribes. He recorded that the "Hudson's Bay Company had sent some young Indian boys to a Protestant school at Red River. Two of these young men came back, one a Spokane and one a Nez Perce, and were the cause that the sacred teachings were spread among the people."[5]

HIS INFLUENCE SPREADS

Every Sunday, Garry would call his tribe together and teach them everything he knew about Christianity, stressing the need for faith in Jesus Christ for forgiveness of sin and for salvation.

Curley Jim, one of Garry's contemporaries, said of the Sunday meetings, "He told us of a God above. He showed us a book, the Bible, from which he read to us. He said to us if we were good, that when we died, we would go up above and see God."[6]

But the influence of the teachings of Garry and Pelly went far beyond their own and neighboring tribes. John McLean, who was at Stuart Lake in the northern part of British Columbia during the winter of 1836, reported, "Two young men, natives of Oregon, who had received a little education at Red River, had, on their return to their own country, introduced a sort of religion whose groundwork seemed to be Christianity. This religion spread with amazing rapidity all over the country. It reached Fort Alexandria, the lower post of the district in the autumn of 1834 or 1835."[7]

The large Nez Perce tribe was greatly influenced by Garry as well. The Reverend A. B. Smith, a worker for the American Board of Commissioners for Foreign Missions among the Nez Perce, wrote:

> About ten years ago, a young Spokane Indian who goes by the name of Spokane Garry, who had been educated at the Red River school, returned. My teacher, the Lawyer, saw him and learned from him the respecting of the Sabbath and some other things which Garry had heard at the school. This was the first that he (Lawyer) had heard about the Sabbath and it was called by the Nez Perce, *Halahpawit*. He returned and communicated what he had heard to his people. Soon after, six of the Nez Perce set out for the States, in search, as he says, of "Christian teachers."[8]

Thus it appears that the famous Nez Perce delegation, which arrived in St. Louis in the fall of 1831, found its inspiration in the teachings of Garry.

The greatest impact of Garry and Pelly on the Indians of the Oregon Country was that they were able to persuade four tribes to send five young men—Kootenay Collins, Spokane Berens, Cayuse Halket and two Nez Perce named Ellis and Pitt—back to the Red River mission school in the spring of 1830. Except for one, all were the sons of chiefs and were between the ages of 12 and 17.[9]

The spread of Christianity throughout the tribes of the Inland Empire is further documented by Washington Irving in *The Adventures of Captain Bonneville*. During the winter of 1832, Bonneville camped with the Nez Perce on the upper Salmon River. From his experiences he reported of the Nez Perce that "simply to call these people religious would convey but a faint idea of the deep hue of piety and devotion which pervades their whole conduct. Their honesty is immaculate and their purity of purpose . . . are most remarkable. They are more like a nation of saints than a horde of savages."[10]

"Their honesty is immaculate and their purity of purpose are most remarkable . . . more like a nation of saints than a horde of savages."

The period of 1835 to 1850 saw the first missionaries come and build missions to teach Christianity to the Indians. The spread of the Word of God during the early 1830s is remarkable in that the first missionaries didn't arrive until late 1835 when Samuel Parker, the first Protestant minister to visit this area, arrived to survey the need for mission work among the Indian tribes of the Northwest.

In the summer of 1836, Henry Harmon Spalding settled at Lapwai near Lewiston, Idaho, among the Nez Perce. Marcus Whitman settled at Waiilaptu near Walla Walla among the Cayuse. In 1838, Elkanah Walker and Cushing Eels established the first Protestant mission among the Spokane tribe. It was here that Garry made a significant contribution to the work of translating parts of the Bible and the Lord's Prayer into the Spokane language. Yet the Reverends Walker and Eels failed to build on the foundations that Garry had established. Having few converts, the mission closed in 1848.

WHAT SHALL WE DO TO BE SAVED?

Washington Territory was rapidly changing. Settlers were moving west and settling the land of the lower Columbia and the Willamette Valley under the terms of the Donation Land Act passed by Congress in 1850. White settlers could acquire 320 acres in the Oregon country at $1.25 an acre. A married couple could purchase 640 acres at the same price.

Tension and conflict between the Spokane Indians and the steadily increasing number of white settlers to the area was growing daily. Blood was spilled in more than one incident. At a council on December 4, 1855, Chief Garry met with White leaders, to whom he appealed for understanding:

> When you look at the red man, you think you have more heart, more sense, than these poor Indians. I think that the difference between us and you Americans is in the clothing; the blood and the body are the same. Do you think that because your mother was white and theirs dark, that

you are higher or better? We are dark, yet if we cut ourselves the blood is red; so with the whites it is the same,
even though their skin is white. I do not think we are poor
if we belong to another nation. If you take the Indians for
men, treat them so now. If you talk to the Indians to make
peace, the Indian will do the same to you.[11]

By the spring of 1870, Chief Garry faced some serious issues
and concerns for his people. Moral decay now prevailed among
the Spokane as a result of the continued sale of whiskey, the
unstable marriages of Indian women whose White husbands frequently deserted them and the growing flow of settlers from
Walla Walla north into Spokane country.

Garry believed there were three things he could do to prevent
the disaster that had already befallen many Native tribes. First,
he started a revival to recall his people to the faith in God that
he had taught them. Second, he established a school to teach
them how to read and write. And third, he determined to secure
a reservation for his people.

In an effort to bring as many members of the tribe as possible together in common worship, Garry launched the revival in
1871. To help him in the preaching of the Word he chose
William Three Mountain, who had been educated by Elkanah
Walker at Tshaimakain and Amamelkan. Garry and William
were successful in arousing new interest in Christianity among
the Spokanes. In order to provide a means of baptism and marriage, he asked the Presbyterian minister Henry H. Spalding for
his help. Spalding had returned to Lapwai in October 1871, after
an absence of 22 years, to minister among the Nez Perce.

Spalding responded to Garry's appeal in May 1873.
Accompanied by 14 Nez Perce helpers, he spent three weeks
among the Spokanes, proclaiming the gospel of Jesus Christ.

Spalding wrote of the time in his memoirs:

> We had a glorious meeting with the Spokane camp. . . .
> God's spirit was present with converting power. The great
> cry was "What shall we do to be saved." 121 on examina-
> tion gave satisfactory evidence of conversion and were
> received into the church. 43 children were baptized.[12]

Garry was pleased with the fruit of Spalding's visit. On July
4, Garry visited him at Kamiah, where Spalding was conducting
a great revival, and urged him to return immediately to Spokane
Falls to preach Christ to another band of Spokanes. Spalding
responded and 38 adults and 9 children were baptized. In
August, Spalding made a third trip to the Spokanes and when he
left, 334 people had been baptized, including 81 children.[13]

In September 1873, Spalding made an unexpected visit to
the Spokanes. With him was Col. E. M. Kemble, government
inspector for Indian Affairs on the Pacific. Spalding had told
Kemble about Garry's education at the Red River mission
school. Kemble was impressed with the industriousness of the
Spokanes and with Chief Garry. He promised to do what he
could to secure a teacher from the Episcopal Church to come
and teach them in the ways of God. Garry wrote a letter for
Kemble to forward to the Episcopal bishop of Oregon and
Washington Territory and to the Missionary Society in New
York. To Garry's dismay, the society was unable to send them a
teacher. Several years passed before the Episcopal Church sent a
teacher to minister to the Spokane people.

The first clergyman of Garry's church, Rev. J. Compton
Burnett, arrived in Spokane Falls early in 1884. Upon his arrival
Burnett bought a section of land on the south of the Little
Spokane River from the Northern Pacific Railroad, and he

immediately dispatched a group of men to begin preparing the land for a crop of oats and potatoes.

The Middle Spokane tribe had cultivated this land for years under the direction of Colonel Watkins of the Indian Service. Watkins and the Indians stopped Burnett's men from beginning to work the land. This infuriated Reverend Burnett; he threatened to report them to the law, charging Watkins with unwarranted interference. This action to deprive the Indians of their lands caused quite a disturbance, and after this incident, Garry never again asked for assistance from the Episcopal Church.

As for Chief Garry's efforts to secure a reservation for his people, a meeting of the Spokane tribe and government officials from the Dawes Commission was held in a livery stable on Riverside Avenue in Spokane Falls, near where the Federal Building is now. Garry, then 67, once again asked for a reservation along the banks of the Spokane River, ancestral lands to the Spokane Indians. There, he said, his people would work the land and practice the teachings of Jesus Christ. He asked the White men to take back their whiskey and their playing cards, the only things they had given the Indians.

Twice before, he had been promised a reservation for his people along the Spokane River. But this final request was immediately denied. By the terms of the commission, the Spokane Indians ceded all their lands lying outside any reservations to the United States and agreed to remove themselves to the Colville, Coeur d'Alene or Jacko Reservations.

PERSONAL DISASTER AND INJUSTICE

Chief Garry and his family lived on a small farm near present day Hillyard on Pleasant Prairie in the city of Spokane, Washington.

He had no intention of giving it up and had asked the Dawes Commission that he be given the opportunity to claim legal ownership of his farm, an opportunity which was granted to him. In order to obtain the title to his farm, he pursued U.S. citizenship. However, before he could obtain citizenship, while he was helping with the annual fishing on the Spokane River in August 1888, word came that Whites had taken possession of his land. Garry and his family hurried home, but he was ordered off his own land by the White men who had taken possession of it. He was permitted to take with him whatever personal possessions he could carry, and then his cabin was burned to the ground.

Garry tried to take his farm back by peaceful and legal means, but blindness to injustice done to an Indian was so characteristic of the times. The U.S. Land Office issued a receipt for the Whites' claim on the land. On August 30, 1888, a loan of $500 was procured by the new owner, probably for the harvesting of the crop that Garry had planted.

Garry was given a hearing on his claim to his farm before U.S. Commissioner Skeel, during which testimony was heard that he and his family had lived on the land for many years and that he was in the process of becoming a citizen of the United States. It was further pointed out that, by becoming a citizen, he would also become a legalized freeholder and, in the meantime, would have squatter's rights and would be protected under the agreement of 1887. At the time of the hearing, the land was valued at $25,000. The matter was taken into consideration.

Having nowhere to live, Garry and his wife, Nina, who was now blind, and their daughter, Nellie, moved their tipi to a place on Latah Creek with the tipis of their friends and relatives. Nellie, in order to take care of her parents, did laundry for the settlers of Spokane Falls. Because Garry was unable to pasture animals on his own land, his horses became easy targets for thieves. Reduced to poverty, he was forced to slaughter his cattle for food.

Ten of the families with whom Garry lived on Latah Creek, tired of living in poor conditions and constant hunger, moved to the Coeur d'Alene Reservation. Others appealed to the Indian agent at Colville for permission to live on the Colville Reservation. Garry continued to live at the site on Latah Creek, where the family was constantly bothered by young vandals who threw rocks at their tipis from the bluff above.

By 1890, the $100-a-year annuity promised in the agreement of 1887 had not found its way into Garry's hand. Aware of Garry's hardship, Mr. Gavin Moaut gave him permission to move his family's campsite to a place in Indian Canyon. There Garry cared for his blind wife and their daughter, who continued to work to provide food for them.

In the fall of 1891, Garry became ill and was unable to carry on. But even in his last days he was not to be left alone by self-seeking Whites. A man came busting into their camp, claiming that if Garry would sign some document and pay him $5 he could get his farm back. No one knows for sure who this man was or what he might have been up to, but Garry told him that he was no longer interested in his farm. He told the man, "I am dying, and all I am thinking of is God. Soon I'll have nothing more to do with this world."[14]

Of one thing there is no doubt. Garry had served his God for many long years "in the testimony of a good conscience; in the confidence of a certain faith; in the comfort of a reasonable, religious and holy hope; in favor with God and perfect charity with all the world."[15] No Christian could ask for more.

Spokane Garry died in his sleep on January 14, 1892. In his hands were his Bible and prayer book, from which he had so often read. Chief Garry had passed to his eternal reward.

A funeral was held on January 16 and was conducted by Reverend Dr. Mundy of the First Presbyterian Church of Spokane. Garry was buried in Greenwood Cemetery, not far from where he had lived, his grave marked by a small wooden cross.

Today there is a plaque in Chief Garry's honor, located at Inspiration Point in Riverfront Park in Spokane, Washington. The inscription reads, "Torn between two cultures as interpreter, peace maker, teacher, and preacher, he was often condemned. Yet his influence cleared the path for the missionaries and eased the way for the settlement of Spokane. He died a forgotten figure in 1892."

CHIEF GARRY'S LEGACY

I have talked with a number of Native leaders from the reservations where Chief Garry's Christian influence and revival had spread in the early days of his ministry. On the five or six reservations where we have conducted casual surveys, we can identify less than two dozen Native men who regularly attend a Protestant church. On the Coeur d'Alene Reservation, 45 miles southeast of Spokane, there are none.

It is hard to imagine what things might be like among the Native people here in the Northwest if the early missionaries, who discovered upon their arrival an already vibrant spiritual awakening, had concluded that God sent them here to come under and support the Native pastors and workers already in place. Instead, what they essentially said was, "You've done a good job, fellas, but we'll take over now." They set themselves up as the true guardians of the faith.

Here were Native Christians who loved Jesus, spoke the language, understood the culture of the people, were already respected and trusted and whose ministries had already born much evident fruit in the way of new believers and growing disciples—and yet they were disrespected and supplanted.

I believe Chief Spokane Garry served the Lord in much the same way as did the apostles Peter, James and John among their people. He walked in apostolic grace as a church planter and father in the faith, teacher of the Word of God, pastoral counselor, fruitful evangelist and shepherd among the sheep. He followed Jesus Christ and laid down his life for his brethren in many situations.

From 1873 to 1876, Spokane Garry kept two journals in which he recorded personal thoughts and some hymns he had taught to his people. The journals included these two hymns:

There is no name so sweet on earth
No name so sweet in heaven
The name before the wondrous birth
To Christ the Savior given.
We love to sing around our King
And hail him blessed Jesus
For there's no word ear ever heard
So dear so sweet as Jesus.[16]

* * * * * *

I am so glad that our Father in heaven
Tells of His love in the book he has given
Wonderful things in the Bible I see
This is the dearest that Jesus loves me
Jesus loves me

Jesus loves even me.

If I forget him and wander away

Still he doth love me wherever I stray

Back to the dear loving arms would I flee

When I remember that Jesus loves me.[17]

Colonel Kemble recorded hearing the Spokanes sing these hymns so sweetly in their camp near the falls. Both hymns indicate Garry's deep devotion to the Savior, about whom he had learned as a young man and to whom he was faithful to the end of his days.

Yet despite his great fruitfulness in the kingdom of God, Garry never found a home in the Body of Christ. He never experienced acceptance, respect, protection and true Christian love from his White brothers and sisters in Christ. He never knew the Church to be a place of equality and mutual service nor, tragically, a place of refuge and haven of peace.

Instead, he was forever and always "just an Indian." He was told his kind did not belong with the White folks. Though people were glad he was a Christian and that his wretched soul was saved from damnation, to most in the Church he was still just an Indian.

Today the northern Idaho and Washington areas have the reputation across the country of being a haven for White supremacists and racist paramilitary camps. I believe the Church, because of the treatment of Spokane Garry and the Native believers in the early history of the area, surrendered this region to a spirit of racial prejudice and pride. It is hard to know what this area would look like spiritually today, particularly among the Native people, had the White Church embraced their Native brethren. I can't help but imagine that things would be much different.

But our future does not need to follow the course set by the attitudes of many of the first settlers and Christians across our nation. We can make a difference. Jesus is calling us by the Spirit to see the kingdom of God come to earth, just as it is in heaven.

> These all died in faith, not having received the promises, but having seen them afar off were assured of them, embraced them and confessed that they were strangers and pilgrims on the earth. For those who say such things declare plainly that they seek a homeland. And truly if they had called to mind that country from which they had come out, they would have had opportunity to return. But now they desire a better, that is, a heavenly country. Therefore God is not ashamed to be called their God, for He has prepared a city for them (Heb. 11:13-16).

Chief Garry deserves a place in any modern account of heroes and heroines of faith. The legacy of peace, faith in Christ and trust in God that his life represents can be a great source of hope and inspiration for the Church in America today.

> And what more shall I say? For the time would fail me to tell of Gideon and Barak and Samson and Jephthah, also of David and Samuel and the prophets: who through faith subdued kingdoms, worked righteousness, obtained promises, stopped the mouths of lions, quenched the violence of fire, escaped the edge of the sword, out of weakness were made strong, became valiant in battle (Heb. 11:32-34).

CHAPTER SEVEN

A WORLD IN NEED OF HEALING

People around me were crying, hugging and praying as I walked up to the young Native man sitting in the church pew. His name was Moses; and he was hunched over with his head in his hands, weeping quietly. He explained to me that he knew if he made a commitment to Jesus Christ it would mean he would have to stop hating White people and learn to love them. He didn't know if he could do that.

In 1994, I was invited by Joe and Punkie Lachnit to be a speaker at a youth outreach called MAD Northwest in Spokane. After a week of training, sharing the gospel and having fun, three teams were formed to travel to the six area reservations for another week of outreach to Native youth.

As the evening speaker, I had just finished leading the young people in a time of prayer and reconciliation. At the conclusion I invited the non-Indian youth to join me in asking the Native youth to forgive them for their own racial prejudice and in acknowledging the sins of their ancestors against Indian people. I then asked the Native youth to join me in asking forgiveness of White youth for their anger, bitterness and unforgiveness toward them. As we brought these issues before the Lord, the Holy Spirit began to impress upon these young people the importance of what was taking place. I then asked if they felt okay to go to someone of the other group to talk and/or pray with them. As they responded, a great deal of repenting, crying and healing took place that night.

Moses was one who came to a crossroads in his life that evening. As we talked, he explained how his mother was in prison; his infant sister had died under very questionable circumstances while in the care of a White foster family; his own family was split up; and he was involved in gangs, drugs and alcohol. He knew that his anger and hatred of White people would probably result in his early death or imprisonment—and he knew he wanted out. That evening he found the Holy Spirit asking him to let it all go. After we talked and cried together, we prayed and Moses was set free in Jesus Christ.

God is bringing His people together in remarkable ways in our generation. Denominational walls, racial walls, gender walls—all are beginning to come down in the Church. We have a long way to go, but we have also come a long way in the past 10 years.

A HOLY VISITATION

In January 1998, my friend Jim Brenn, pastor of Skyline Foursquare Church, held his second missions conference in Anchorage, Alaska. Part of the vision for the conference was to work through some reconciliation issues among the Alaskan Native and non-Native brethren and to gain new understanding of the role of Native people relative to God's purposes for Alaska and beyond.

Something very powerful occurred at this conference on a Tuesday afternoon after I taught on the value of the cultural giftings and on the grace of Native people in God's redemptive purposes for the nations. At the close of my presentation, I showed an 18-minute video on the inaugural World Christian Gathering of Indigenous People that had been held in New Zealand in 1996. The video contained highlights from the eight-day gathering of indigenous believers from 32 countries, each group worshiping Jesus with its own unique cultural music, songs, dancing and attire.

At the conclusion of the video, a beautiful song of reflection was sung, talking about the returning of the indigenous peoples in dignity, strength, hope, courage and purity and their walking in the light and praising God because their deliverer had come. While the music played, the video showed aboriginal peoples, including a few North American Natives, dancing, praying and worshiping in various traditional cultural expressions. As the video drew to a close, I heard a few people behind me gently weeping. Slowly, the sound of their weeping increased; and I could feel the wounding and deep heart cry of the Native people in the room, including my own.

By the time the video ended and the credits were rolling, nearly everyone in the room was crying. No one even bothered to turn off the video player. I too began to cry and was soon undone, head in hands, sobbing from a deep place of loss and identification with the pain of Native people. Men and women alike began to wail and lament loudly, as though they were at a funeral. Soon the room was filled with the weighty presence of the Spirit of God, accompanied by deep intercession with groanings—Native and White were groaning together in travail. This holy time of visitation by God among His people went on for 15 to 20 minutes. It was a time of healing of souls and release from hurt and loss for Native people.

This was a bittersweet experience because there was a sense of deep loss and, at the same time, overwhelming joy at the return of something of great value that had been lost. Some then began to speak words of prophecy. As this time ended, I asked a few Native folks to come up and try to explain what had just happened to all of us.

People said that when they saw the Native people in the video dancing, they wanted to be free to do the same thing but felt the loss of not being able to. Several said they saw in the video what they themselves had longed for in their own lives but were afraid to try for fear of persecution from the Church. One lady said how bad she felt at the sight of others enjoying the freedom to worship in their cultural forms, a freedom they themselves had never known. An Athabascan woman expressed great sadness because, when the missionaries came to her village, the Church had taken away their dances and now they couldn't remember how to do them anymore.

One individual said he felt the Lord was giving back to them the Native culture that the devil had stolen and had attempted to destroy. As these things were shared, there was much agreement and affirmation among the people and a distinct sense of joyful hope being restored. Many of these Alaska Natives were, in their words, "set free to be Native again." This time of visitation and healing served to lay the foundation for a powerful time of reconciliation.

THEY DANCED WITH ALL THEIR MIGHT

At the conclusion of the conference on Thursday night, an Eskimo brother named Joe, a well-known traditional Native dancer in his youth, was set free to dance again after many years of repression by the Church. He had been writing new Eskimo dances and worship songs to Jesus for more than a year and was only now finding the freedom to use them before his brethren. Traditional Eskimo drums were used to worship Jesus, and almost everyone in the assembly, one by one, came up to play the drum, each being set free as he or she began to play.

Reconciliation occurred when Whites, too, were invited up on the platform to strike the drum, because the Native brothers felt this new blessing to worship should be shared with all. The Anglo brethren who had for so long condemned the use of traditional instruments and dance were now expressing their repentance by joining in with their Native brethren to play the drum, thus affirming the value of these cultural expressions. In a very real way they were returning or restoring cultural expressions to their rightful owners in the name of the Lord.

People worshiped, sang and danced until after midnight. Many people were powerfully released to express their love for God in praise as true biblical reconciliation was being acted out beyond the beginning stage of right words!

I have witnessed this scene repeated many times across the land among people of different cultures, ethnic backgrounds, religious affiliations and gender differences, almost always with the same wonderful results. People are looking for ways out of the destructive cycle of blame, unforgiveness, hatred and bitterness. Only Jesus can lead us out, into the promised land of reconciliation.

From Adam and Eve's disobedience and consequential expulsion from the Garden to Cain's murder of Abel, from the peoples of the earth being scattered at Babel until now, human beings have been in need of being reconciled to God and to one another. All creation is waiting for liberation, freedom, a return to its original state of sinless existence with the Creator (see Rom. 8:18-23).

WORDS WITHOUT WORKS

Reconciliation is the healing and restoring of divided or broken relationships. It is only in the fertile seedbed of repentance that true reconciliation can find life. Biblical repentance is always a turning away from a former way and turning to God, authenticated by actions. There should always be tangible evidence when true biblical reconciliation takes place between fallen man and his Creator as well as between estranged people or people groups. In simplest terms, no change of behavior toward a relationship means no reconciliation!

After teaching in Edmonton, I was told by a Cree woman named Ann that she had always had a nagging question in her heart about whether or not God fully loved her. Sobbing, she told me that she doubted God's complete love because she was a Cree Indian. After listening to me teach, she believed for the first time that God fully loved her and that she no longer needed to be ashamed of her Cree identity.

I pastored a predominantly White church for 13 years in Vancouver, Washington. Having been teamed with my non-Native brethren in ministry for nearly 18 years, I have at least a little understanding about how some Anglo Christians view Native Americans in a cultural as well as Christian context. If I were a spiritual optometrist, I would say that in the area of cross-cultural sensitivity and awareness, many people suffer serious cases of impaired vision. Sometimes I find a confused mixture of culture and gospel. Some identify the abundance of America and her free-market economy, democracy, capitalism and even the injustices of "manifest destiny" as necessarily being Christian or being God's will. There has been little effort in this nation to get inside the minds of Native or ethnic peoples in order to genuinely understand and empathize with their pain and experiences. Native American history is viewed with very little compassion; as a result there is still estrangement between Anglo and Native people and their cultures.

I am encouraged as I see God raising up strong prophetic voices among our Anglo brethren. For instance, Bill McCartney of Promise Keepers has issued a challenge to White believers to learn to share in the pain of their African-American, Hispanic, Native American and Oriental brothers. I say, "Amen!" to Mr. McCartney's challenge for men all over this country to begin meeting on a monthly basis across denominational and racial lines as a first step toward reconciliation and biblical unity.

In a conversation I had with C. Peter Wagner at a conference in Seoul, South Korea, he concurred that racism is easily the most crippling disease infecting the Church today. Now it seems God is opening our hearts to Him in brokenness, repentance and forgiveness, for our own sin as well as for the sins of our fathers.

ALL ARE GUILTY

For our part as Native American Christians, we need to genuinely extend to those who ask, forgiveness for the sins and injustices of their forefathers. Bitterness, anger and blame resulting from unforgiveness will only keep us divided as cohabitants of this land and will destroy our people. We must resist the devil by reminding ourselves that despite the mistakes and cultural blunders of many early and present-day missionaries among our people, without their efforts we would still be in great darkness without Christ.

If Natives had canoed across the Atlantic and discovered Europe, Europeans would probably all be wearing buckskins and leathers today. I have no doubt that, had the roles been reversed, we would have been no less ethnocentric and brutal than the Whites who came here from France, Holland, England, Spain, etc. We must continually ask the Holy Spirit to anoint our hands with oil so we won't be able to hold on too tightly to the wrongs of the past.

Another concern among Native Christians is to see our old tribal and clan disputes resolved and bitterness healed. Many of our tribes are historically bitter enemies. As Native people we must also own up to the fact that our people committed many heinous acts of violence against innocent White settlers and homesteaders. For example, in the Whitman massacre of 1847 near Walla Walla, Washington, 14 dedicated White missionaries were killed by a Cayuse raiding party.

We must also allow the Lord to call us to prayer and to use us to break demonic strongholds of hatred, violence and unforgiveness. Much is being written and discussed about the Church's role and responsibility concerning reconciliation and healing for the sins enacted against Native people by White people and vice versa. New territory is being explored in identifying demonic strongholds and how to tear them down. Native Americans, as the indigenous people of this land, have been identified by prophetic individuals in the Church as being in some way inseparably linked to spiritual revival in the Americas.

In light of the growing prophetic and intercessory prayer movements, I find myself growing in faith and hope that these endeavors will bear fruit and give evidence to the realities of biblical reconciliation, not only between Natives and Whites, but among all of God's people everywhere.

HEALING FOR THE NATIONS

In 1994, at an international prayer conference in Seoul, South Korea, I witnessed the awesome power of reconciliation between people groups. An Anglo brother from America, Tom White, stood with me before a gathering of more than 300 Christian leaders from 43 countries of the world. He asked me to forgive him for the injustices that White people had enacted against the Native people of the Americas. I forgave him and also asked forgiveness for the bitterness, resentment and hatred that many of our people have felt toward White people. This event served to trigger an avalanche of reconciliation between peoples in the following days and changed my life forever!

The next morning, a Japanese brother asked attendees from the Philippines, Korea, China, Malaysia, Taiwan and Indonesia to forgive the sins of Japan for her cruelty and destruction inflicted on their people during World War II. A sixth-generation Dutch Afrikaner woman from South Africa asked Black brethren from Africa to forgive South Africa for the sins of apartheid, and she then began to wash the feet of one of the men. One African brother asked the Black brethren from America to join them on the stage. He asked their forgiveness for the many Black African tribal chiefs, their great grandparents and forefathers, who had sold their fellow tribesmen and children into slavery. As I witnessed these acts of reconciliation, the presence of God overwhelmed me, and I found myself sobbing unashamedly before the Lord, my heart broken in repentance and joy. All of us wept and then rejoiced as we partook in that incredible move of the Spirit for repentance and reconciliation.

Jesus didn't tell us that to practice a truth we have to understand it intellectually first. He didn't tell us to understand His Word and then do it. He said *do* my Word (see John 14:23; Jas. 1:22). I've found that understanding often comes as the result of doing, not the reverse. So despite my rational and theological struggles with the how-to of genuine, biblical, racial reconciliation, I cast my lot as a fellow pilgrim to practice the Word in simple obedience and to be a part of the solution rather than a part of the problem.

God must be at the center of

the affairs of men on this

earth. Without Him, we

cannot walk in harmony.

JESUS IS THE KEY TO BUILDING RELATIONSHIPS

Because all successful human relationships are, by design, trinitarian in nature, no two people can walk in harmony without God's third-party involvement. A successful relationship or friendship requires the cooperation of you, your friend and Jesus. The same holds true on a national level. Nations may enjoy degrees of civil cooperation, but no two nations can enter into fullness of unity without Jesus.

Why? Because God must be at the center of the affairs of men on this earth. Jesus said in John 15:5, "Without Me you can do nothing." That includes loving and getting along.

Without Him, we simply can't do it.

This brings us to the issue of reconciliation and the unique role of God's people as bearers of the message of reconciliation. We can bring healing because Jesus has freed us to be self-sacrificially honest. We were reconciled to God through honest confession, and we reconcile people to people in the same way.

I ask you to please take some time to pray, to meditate and to ask the Lord about the following insights offered by John Dawson in his book *Healing America's Wounds:*

> The greatest wounds in human history, the greatest injustices, have not happened through the acts of some individual perpetrator, but rather through the institutions, systems, philosophies, cultures, religions and governments of mankind. Because of this we, as individuals, are tempted to absolve ourselves of all individual responsibility.
>
> Unless somebody identifies themselves with corporate entities, such as the nation of our citizenship or the subculture of our ancestors, the act of honest confession will never take place. This leaves us in a world of injury and offense in which no corporate sin is ever acknowledged, reconciliation never begins and old hatreds deepen.[1]

It seems to me that there is an order to the process of reconciliation. First, there is acknowledgment of injustice, or sin, that produces sorrow in the souls of men. Second, that sorrow, if allowed to go deeper, produces godly remorse. Third, if that person remains open, the Holy Spirit can take remorse deeper yet, giving birth to repentance. It is only in the fertile seedbed of repentance that true reconciliation can find life.

DEALING WITH HISTORICAL SINS AND INJUSTICES

The peoples of the world are deeply wounded and tormented by unresolved offenses and guilt. As we have seen, much of this wounding is the result of clashing worldview distinctives.

Human beings created in the image of God are designed for the purpose of walking in harmony with their Creator. This is a reconciled life. Because of sin, people and nations are both victims and victimizers and are therefore guilty of all manner of abuse, selfishness, injury and separation. The world is in an impossible deadlock, and First Nations peoples are no exception.

As First Nations people, we struggle and wrestle with a number of issues related to political and social oppression, as well as cultural and spiritual injustices. One that will be covered in greater detail later but that is still worth mentioning here is the breaking of covenants. Broken covenants have had an enormous negative impact on the relationship between Native Americans and the U.S. government. Historically, broken covenants have caused a huge chasm of distrust and great animosity in the hearts of Native people.

So what do we do about the past? Chalk it up as history and simply move on? Some might say, "Come on, that's water under the bridge. What's done is done and we can't change it now, so let's just forget the past and get on with life."

I see a tension in our understanding of the Scriptures between all things becoming new and old things passing away (see 2 Cor. 5:17) and the sins of the fathers being passed down to the succeeding generations (see Exod. 20:5,6; Num. 14:18,19).

Some would say that as Christians we should not dwell on the sins of the past but only on the present and future. Others would say that unless we deal with the sins of the past, our offenses will be passed on to each succeeding generation, as has been the case with Ireland, Bosnia, Rwanda and the First Nations.

As an example of how an offense has a life of its own—a mental stronghold of sorts—consider the fact that the source of the conflict and animosity in Bosnia/Herzogevena goes back at least to the fourteenth century. Hatred has been passed to each succeeding generation through a minimum of five or six centuries. This means that cultural prejudices and offenses are now hundreds of years old, and each generation has picked them up and carried them for the duration of their lives, only to see their children and grandchildren do the same.

As fully devoted followers and disciples of Jesus Christ, we can step into long-standing deadlocks as agents of healing between Native and Anglo cultures. As we clearly see and acknowledge the sins of our nations *(ethnos)* of origin, we in the Church must learn to identify with those nations and people before the Lord—not as some long-ago people having nothing to do with us, but *as our own*. We must come to understand that our human corporateness means that our forefathers' sins are *our* sins. We must learn to live out the biblical practice of prayer with identification (see, for example, Dan. 9). This type of prayer and intercession has incredible potential to bring revival and healing to all the inhabitants of America, but it has remained a neglected truth.

Many of the great prayer warriors of the Bible approached God with a sense of shame and embarrassment for the sins and wickedness of their forefathers. They did not disassociate themselves from their ancestors' sins, nor did they try to absolve themselves from all sense of personal responsibility for the resultant condition of their nation. Instead, they faced with stark honesty the corruption around them and owned it as theirs. They identified with their nation's sinful history as their present-day responsibility.

We can identify with the sins of our nation in both personal and corporate repentance. I believe and have seen in many situations that prayers of identification can tear down the walls of division and racial strife and open hearts to Christ in new, deep and profound ways.

Unless we deal with the roots of sin that have oppressed First Nations people and thereby darkened the history of our nation, revival will not come to our land. Why? Because the roots of these sins grant demonic powers the right to accomplish many evils. Only through copious and consistent repentance can strongholds of the enemy be torn down and freedom come.

Nehemiah is a great study in praying with identification. Though Nehemiah had never lived in Jerusalem and did not personally contribute to its spiritual condition, he prayed, "Both my father's house and I have sinned" (Neh. 1:6). Like Nehemiah, we must identify with the wrongs of our country and own them as they relate to the oppression of Native peoples. We are all in this thing together!

As believers we must employ the same tools that Nehemiah utilized. Repentance, confession, forgiveness, reconciliation and restitution were his instruments of reconciliation; and they must be ours if we are to restore this land.

RELATIONSHIP AS THE FOUNDATION

As an active member of the International Reconciliation Coalition, I have heard enough firsthand reports from reconcilers across the world that I am convinced that nothing significant will happen in the way of reconciliation without honest, Christ-honoring and truly loving relationships. Our relationships and friendships in Christ Jesus, which are to be built on trust and mutual respect for one another, are the building blocks of healing in the world. I have worked with the Northwest Regional Task Force on Racial Reconciliation for Promise Keepers, and we see building relationships as the key to healing and building trust in our Native communities.

I once heard a preacher say that the greatest evangelistic text in the Bible is found in Jesus' words in John 17:20,21 (*NIV*):

> My prayer is not for them alone. I pray also for those who will believe in me through their message, that all of them may be one, Father, just as you are in me and I am in you. May they also be in us so that the world may believe that you have sent me.

It is from observing the quality of our relationships with one another that non-Christians will arrive at the conclusion that there is reality in Jesus Christ. How awesome it will be when skeptical non-Christian Natives are moved by envy at the sight of Native and Anglo folks loving, preferring, honoring, enjoying and serving one another!

I have witnessed relationships serving as the basis for reconciliation, as well as relationships arising from reconciliation. Regardless of which comes first, our relationships are the bridges that will endure and over which great, loving armies of ministry can flow both ways—to and from God's First Nations people.

THE BLACK WHITE MAN

An offbeat, western comedy titled *Little Big Man* was released in the early 1970s. In one scene Jack, a young White man who was adopted as a boy by Cheyenne Indians, attempts to explain to an old chief about Black men. Jack describes them as having black skin and wooly black hair. He says they fought with the U.S. Calvary and were called Buffalo Soldiers. The old chief, who has never seen a Black man, says, "Yes, I have heard of them. They are the Black White men."[2]

This accurately expresses the attitudes of many western tribes who, having no historical frame of reference to place Blacks as descendants of Africa, saw them as a different kind of White man. I don't pretend to know or even understand the reasons and history of it, but there is tension and, at times, outright prejudice among many Native people toward African-Americans.

One morning in Portland, Oregon, five of us Native pastors and leaders were having coffee after our regular prayer time. As we were talking, Harvey Hood, a Klamath Indian pastor, shared a perplexing and bothersome incident that had happened the previous week. Harvey had recently started a home church at the residence of a Native family and had invited an African-American brother to come and speak to this home fellowship the previous Saturday evening. Before he finished telling the story, the rest of us were smiling knowingly, anticipating the conclusion. Harvey said that the family in whose home the meeting was held had told him that if African-Americans would be coming, they didn't want the meetings at their home any longer. Others in the home group had also expressed some discomfort.

Harvey asked why we were smiling. One of the pastors asked Harvey if he was aware that many Native folks are uncomfortable with African-Americans. This led to a discussion as to why this might be true, with each of us sharing personal experiences and stories.

STRAINED RELATIONS BETWEEN AFRICANS AND NATIVE AMERICANS

In the early history of the United States, runaway slaves were readily welcomed by many eastern tribes, even sheltered and adopted and often accepted as marriage partners. As a result many African-American people today have Native blood, and many First Nations people, particularly in the East, have African blood.

On the other side of the coin, a few tribes that had been relocated to the Oklahoma Indian country owned and kept black slaves. Though it was a short-lived episode, nonetheless it is a part of those tribes' history.

I have heard many Native people express anger or distrust with and alienation from the African-American community. It was explained to me that during the civil rights movement against racial injustice, African-Americans never included Native people in their struggle, even though we protected and fought for them in the early days of our common history.

At the 1996 Promise Keepers clergy conference in Atlanta, I had very insightful conversations with two African-American brothers. One approached me out of the blue to share his experiences and to ask forgiveness for his neglect of his Native American brethren. The other told me a story of an incident involving him and a Native man near the Wind River Reservation in Wyoming.

Wanting to contribute to the Native community, my Black brother had offered to train and assist a young Native woman in his employ, so that she could start her own hair salon. When the young woman asked her father for his approval, he refused. Wondering if the father had misunderstood his intentions or if he had offended the girl's father in some way, my Black friend asked to speak to him. After some conversation, in an attempt to establish rapport with the Native father, he remarked, as one man of color to another, "After all, we're brothers." The Native man replied, "No! We are *not* brothers."

The African-American then quoted Martin Luther King, Jr., as having said that he would fight injustice among all people wherever it was found. The Native man retorted that, despite what King promised, Black people had never included Native people in their fight for civil rights. The young woman's father then abandoned the conversation. The African-American man has never forgotten the Native's remarks.

An African-American army chaplain approached me and two of my Native brothers as we were standing and talking at the conclusion of the Promise Keepers clergy conference. As he stood with us in his full dress uniform, he began to weep as he shared how he was convicted and challenged because of his own lack of awareness, concern and regard for his Native brethren. He asked us to forgive him, and we prayed for one another. Then he asked my Native brothers if they would each please remove one of his chaplain's crosses from his lapel. He asked if I would take one of his U.S. pins from his uniform. He then asked us to let them be reminders of one African-American's new love and commitment to his Native brethren. To this day I wear that pin.

As the family of God, we are being called to bring healing to these divisions among cultures and people groups and to demonstrate to the world a power and grace to walk with one another in true honor and respect, declaring that there is a better way—the Jesus Way.

CHAPTER EIGHT

BROKEN TREATIES HAVE CONSEQUENCES

With the hot afternoon sun adding to his already considerable discomfort at being posted on watch, the uneasy sentry could make out what appeared to be about a dozen of the "renegade" Indians approaching the fort on horseback. Because of recent skirmishes, the tension in and around the fort that day was like a steel trap ready to snap.

The lead horseman was holding the flag of truce, a white cloth tied to the end of a stick, which was flapping in the hot afternoon breeze. He was followed into the fort by a handful of mounted warriors, riding single file, slowly, cautiously. Gen. George Wright had called for a truce and had invited the Indians to the fort on the Spokane River in eastern Washington to discuss a peaceful solution to the fighting.

Once inside the walls, shock and fear gripped the riders as they were seized and disarmed by a large number of soldiers who had been in hiding. Confused and captured, the Natives could only follow where they were led. General Wright ordered them taken to the gallows. Realizing the trap had snapped shut on them, they began to sing their haunting death chants. Without discussion, trial or regard for law, the Natives were promptly, unceremoniously and illegally hung on the spot. This approach to negotiations with the local tribes was how Wright came to be known throughout the territory as "the hanging general." Today the former military post in present-day Spokane is named in his honor—Fort Wright.

The breaking of treaties, or covenants, has caused a huge chasm of distrust and great animosity in the hearts of Native people toward Whites. The U.S. government broke more than 98 percent of all the hundreds of treaties—signed and ratified by Congress—made with the sovereign First Nations of North America. Rev. Silas Correa of the Otoe Nation, a respected Native Christian leader, has said, along with many others, that of the more than 800 treaties made, not one was kept!

These broken covenants have not only left a natural alienation between people groups but also have loaded America with a national spiritual indebtedness toward Native people and the Lord God Himself. It is not at all unlikely, from a biblical perspective, that God may summon America to give an account for her unethical, immoral and illegal covenant-breaking history in dealing with Native peoples.

A FAITHFUL GOD, A FAITHLESS PEOPLE

I want to present a point of view that these broken covenants are a possible contributing factor in the spiritual decline of America as a nation. Covenant breaking is one of the identifying characteristics of a person or people given to rebellion, ungodliness or disobedience. The sin of covenant breaking is one of the conditions to which God relinquishes His people because of their rejection of who He is:

> They have become filled with every kind of wickedness, evil, greed and depravity. They are full of envy, murder, strife, deceit and malice. They are gossips, slanderers, God-haters, insolent, arrogant and boastful; they invent ways of doing evil; they disobey their parents; they are senseless, faithless, heartless, ruthless. Although they know God's righteous decree that those who do such things deserve death, they not only continue to do these very things but also approve of those who practice them (Rom. 1:29-32, *NIV*).

"Faithless" in this passage is translated from the Greek *asunthetos*, meaning "not agreed" or "treacherous to compacts." In the *King James Version* this word is translated "covenant breakers."

All true believers are in covenant with God through Jesus Christ and the New Covenant. They are also in covenant relationship with each other. Our Christian covenant contains some good tools for us to use for walking in unity and breaking down barriers and walls between brethren.

The specific purpose of divine covenants is to be a primary means of communicating—and fulfilling—God's will and purpose for man. From His first covenant with Adam, all God's covenants have revealed and expressed His desire and intention to have loving relationships with people. I believe a primary influence, emphasis and focus of our covenant in Christ should be its power to produce unity and oneness among His people. Unity as seen in lasting relationships among Christians is the highest form of evangelism. Jesus prayed "that they all may be one . . . that the world may believe that You sent Me" (John 17:21).

Making and keeping covenants reveal many aspects of the nature of our Creator. Our heavenly Father makes, keeps, initiates and enables covenant; therefore, as His people, so should we.

A Covenant-Making God

Throughout the Scriptures we see God entering into covenant with His people:

- **Adamic Covenant.** Made before the entrance of sin by Adam and Eve, this covenant reveals God's original purposes for the whole of Adam's race (see Gen. 1,2).
- **Abrahamic Covenant.** Made with Abraham, the father of all who believe, this covenant involved Abraham, his natural and national seed called Israel and the Messianic seed, Jesus Christ. It includes prophetically the entrance not only of believing Israelites but also of Gentiles into the kingdom of God (see Gen. 15:18-21; 17:2-5).
- **Mosaic Covenant.** Made strictly and only with the chosen nation of Israel at the foot of Mount Sinai after the exodus from Egypt, this covenant was not made with any Gentile nations but rather pointed Israel to the Christ who would be the Savior of the world (see Gal. 3:24).
- **The New Covenant.** Made by the Lord Jesus Christ, this covenant became the fulfillment of all previous covenants, abolishing in itself their temporal elements and making possible their everlasting elements.

The New Covenant brings every believer into everlasting covenant (see Heb. 8:6-13; 9:15).

A Covenant-Keeping God

God reveals His faithfulness and trustworthiness in that He keeps all covenants He makes. Once God has made a covenant, He does not forget it nor does he neglect it. He always follows through with the commitments He has made.

Historically, among most North American tribes, giving your word was sacred. As Christians, our word should be even more trustworthy because it is based on a better and greater covenant. Sadly, that isn't always the case.

In biblical times the word "covenant" involved promise, commitment, faithfulness and loyalty, even unto death. A covenant was sacred and was not lightly entered into by the parties involved. A person was only as good as his covenant word. The same is still true among First Nations people today.

A Covenant-Revealing God

In order for man to be in covenant relationship with Him, God had to reveal the covenant to man, openly declaring the promise and terms. Apart from God's taking the initiative and revealing His covenant to us, we would have remained ignorant of the availability of covenantal relationship with Him.

A Covenant-Enabling God

The same God who makes, keeps and reveals His covenants to us also enables us to fulfill our part of the covenant. Man has proven his inability to keep the terms of any covenant without the enabling grace of God (see Rom. 7). This was particularly illustrated under the Mosaic Covenant (see Eph. 2:4-13).

FAMINE IN THE LAND

There are several ways to look at the following story as an example of both the convenantal and redemptive nature of our Father. Redemptively, it is an example of how God is able to use our worst blunders for His glory, as He did with King David. From a covenant perspective, the story reveals how powerful covenants (and treaties) between people really are:

> When the people of Gibeon heard what Joshua had done to Jericho and Ai, they resorted to a ruse: They went as a delegation whose donkeys were loaded with worn-out sacks and old wineskins, cracked and mended. The men put worn and patched sandals on their feet and wore old clothes. All the bread of their food supply was dry and moldy. Then they went to Joshua in the camp at Gilgal and said to him and the men of Israel, "We have come from a distant country; make a treaty with us. . . . Our elders and all those living in our country said to us, 'Take provisions for your journey; go and meet them and say to them, "We are your servants; make a treaty with us." ' This bread of ours was warm when we packed it at home on the day we left to come to you. But now see how dry and moldy it is. And these wineskins that we filled were new, but see how cracked they are. And our clothes and sandals are worn out by the very long journey."
>
> The men of Israel sampled their provisions but did not inquire of the LORD. Then Joshua made a treaty of

peace with them to let them live, and the leaders of the assembly ratified it by oath. Three days after they made the treaty with the Gibeonites, the Israelites heard that they were neighbors, living near them. So the Israelites set out and on the third day came to their cities: Gibeon, Kephirah, Beeroth and Kiriath Jearim. But the Israelites did not attack them, because the leaders of the assembly had sworn an oath to them by the LORD, the God of Israel. The whole assembly grumbled against the leaders, but all the leaders answered, "We have given them our oath by the LORD, the God of Israel, and we cannot touch them now. This is what we will do to them: We will let them live, so that wrath will not fall on us for breaking the oath we swore to them" (Josh. 9:3-6,11-20, *NIV*).

Four centuries later,

During the reign of David, there was a famine for three successive years; so David sought the face of the LORD. The LORD said, "It is on account of Saul and his blood-stained house; it is because he put the Gibeonites to death." The king summoned the Gibeonites and spoke to them. (Now the Gibeonites were not a part of Israel but were survivors of the Amorites; the Israelites had sworn to spare them, but Saul in his zeal for Israel and Judah had tried to annihilate them.) David asked the Gibeonites, "What shall I do for you? How shall I make amends so that you will bless the LORD's inheritance?"

The Gibeonites answered him, "We have no right to demand silver or gold from Saul or his family, nor do we have the right to put anyone in Israel to death."

BROKEN TREATIES HAVE CONSEQUENCES   183

"What do you want me to do for you?" David asked.

They answered the king, "As for the man who destroyed us and plotted against us so that we have been decimated and have no place anywhere in Israel, let seven of his male descendants be given to us to be killed and exposed before the LORD at Gibeah of Saul—the LORD's chosen one."

So the king said, "I will give them to you."

David brought the bones of Saul and his son Jonathan from there, and the bones of those who had been killed and exposed were gathered up. They buried the bones of Saul and his son Jonathan in the tomb of Saul's father Kish, at Zela in Benjamin, and did everything the king commanded. After that, God answered prayer in behalf of the land (2 Sam. 21:1-6,13,14, *NIV*).

There are some intriguing points to consider in this story, an illustration of the importance of covenants.

- Joshua and the congregational leaders did not ask the Lord if He wanted them to make this treaty/covenant with the Gibeonites.
- God did not initiate or design this covenant. It was not a divinely inspired agreement. It had nothing to with God in its inception or completion.
- This treaty was entered into by the government representatives of two sovereign nations.
- It was a covenant based on lies, deceit and fraud.
- The Gibeonites were a foreign nation, outside of God's covenant family.
- From a humanitarian point of view it was an honorable and commendable covenant.

- Though it was not a God-initiated covenant, the leaders realized that they could not break it because God would hold them accountable for breaking their covenantal word.
- Even though God did not initiate or design it, He still enforced it.
- It remained intact for 400 years. It was not dissolved over time.
- When Saul broke the conditions of the Gibeonite covenant, God judged Israel with a three-year drought and famine.
- God judged the entire nation for one man's wrongdoing. Saul was the king of a nation, more than a president or prime minister, and in this political office he brought judgment on the populace by his decision.
- The judgment came several years after Saul's death.
- God judged the generation of Israelites who were 13 generations removed from the time in which Joshua made the covenant.
- The generation on whom the judgment fell had done nothing wrong to incur this judgment upon themselves and their children.
- God refused to answer the prayers of Israel because of this broken treaty.
- Restitution could only be made by appropriate representatives of the offending nation.
- Restitution was defined and determined by the offended nation.
- Only after restitution had been made by the offending nation did God answer the prayers of Israel "on behalf of the land" (2 Sam 21:14, *NIV*).

Is America under this same type of judgment today? My supposition, based upon the biblical concept of covenant, is that the United States of America may very well be held to give an accounting for her broken treaties with the First Nations people of North America.

Few will disagree that America is struggling spiritually. With violence in the schools, increased social dysfunction, economic concerns, decreasing church attendance, shrinking financial giving and political animosity, one must wonder about the apparent loss of spiritual power and influence of the Church in this land.

What is the Spirit of the Lord saying to the Church in America about the sins of her forefathers?

It is reasonable to think that given the immeasurable storehouse of Christian information available—books, cassettes, Sunday sermons, radio and television programs, Bible schools and seminaries, videos, etc.—the Church should instead be rapidly attaining some proportional levels of spiritual maturity and growth. Some Christians—though as yet, all too few—are genuinely inquiring of the Lord, asking if the Gibeonite precedent is what is happening in America today.

Had David not heard from the Lord during a time of prayer and intercession for Israel, neither he nor the nation would likely have ever made the connection between the famine and the breaking of the Gibeonite covenant. I doubt that without the aid of the Holy Spirit it would ever enter our own thinking to make the connection between America's broken covenants with Native

American sovereign nations and our current spiritual and moral decline. Perhaps it's time to consider what the Spirit of the Lord may be saying to the Church in America today about the sins her forefathers committed in breaking hundreds of treaties with the Gibeonites of this land.

MAKING THE CONNECTION

Even before the Europeans came, we as Native people were divided and at war with each other. The Shawnee chief Tecumseh nearly pulled together a multitribal military alliance to fight the Europeans; but in the end the tribes were scattered and Tecumseh was killed.

There is a spirit of competition and division in the land that preceded the arrival of the Europeans—a spiritual stronghold that often plagues Native Christian leaders even today. We are far too quick to pull others down, defend our perceived ministerial territories or constituencies, fight for funding and compete for recognition and position in ministry. I believe the tools of covenant building—whether used to build bridges between White and Native, White and White or Native and Native—can help equip us to overcome many of the long-standing barriers in the Body of Christ by promoting Christ-honoring relationships among all believers.

Covenants demand humility. We must consider Paul's words about not being spiritually high-minded and remembering that it was through the Jews that the gospel of Christ came to the rest of us (see Rom. 11:17-21). Native people, despite the mistakes and abuses of early White missionaries, need to appreciate the fact that it was still those Whites whom God chose to send to us. Gratitude need not blind us to offenses that need to be forgiven; but gratitude and forgiveness are prerequisites for humility.

WE ARE ALL COVENANT PARTNERS

One day the Lone Ranger and Tonto were riding across the prairie. Suddenly, a large war party of Indians surprised them from the east. Quickly they rode down a ravine from the east and came up on the west side only to be met by another war party. They rode back into the ravine and experienced the same thing to the north and south. Realizing they were surrounded by Indians on the warpath, the Lone Ranger turned to Tonto and said, "What are we going to do?" Pausing as he assessed their predicament, Tonto replied, "What do you mean *we*, White Man?"

In 1 Corinthians 12:26 Paul wrote, "And if one member suffers, all the members suffer with it; or if one member is honored, all the members rejoice with it." As we see in the book of Acts, throughout the Early Church there was a sense of oneness, a connectedness that resulted in a quality of mutual care and concern that isn't often seen today. As we have seen, Native cultures also practiced a connected and integrated community lifestyle, but that was not part of the White culture that came to them. Sadly, a sense of connectedness is becoming more and more difficult for Native people to maintain as White culture threatens to overrun and displace the Native way. Today, regardless of culture, personal achievement or success is what drives the majority of individuals, local churches and organizations. Growth, size, buildings and conversions are measuring devices to determine how well we're doing. Less and less do we measure of our relationships by how well we are connected with and caring for one another.

Most pastors rarely take the time to consider how their fellow pastors and churches in the city are doing. During my 13 years of pastoral experience it seemed to me that this was often more true of pastors of large churches. Granted, it takes a lot of time and energy to give leadership to a large congregation. However, because growth is the fruit of God's grace, this blessing carries with it a degree of responsibility to move beyond self-propagation and sustained growth; it requires coming alongside and assisting fellow believers in smaller churches.

I believe the same is true of people groups. Some have come into their own promised land, while others have not. After five centuries Native peoples have yet to fully realize their inheritance in the evangelical mainstream of the Church in North America, while to a larger degree our Anglo, Hispanic and African-American brothers and sisters have.

The following story of the children of Israel's journey helps illustrate this dynamic. In chapter 32 of the book of Numbers we find the children of Israel coming out of the wilderness to take the Promised Land. They have just destroyed and taken the land and its possessions from the Midianites on the east side of the Jordan. This former territory of the Midianites was great pastureland. The tribes of Reuben and Gad were ranchers with very large herds, and they wanted to settle the lands of Djazair and Gilead for their families and herds. They wanted to stay in this land and not go with the other tribes across the Jordan into Canaan. The Lord became angry with them for their selfishness and lack of concern for their brethren's welfare. Moses said to the Gadites and Reubenites, "Shall your countrymen go to war while you sit here? Why do you discourage the Israelites from going over into the land the LORD has given them?" (Num. 32:6,7, *NIV*). The tribes of Reuben and Gad then had a change of heart and repented, saying:

We are ready to arm ourselves and go ahead of the
Israelites until we have brought them to their place. . . .
We will not return to our homes until every Israelite has
received his inheritance (Num. 32:17,18, *NIV*).

One of the intriguing dynamics of this biblical account lies
in how the two tribes forgot their connectedness for a moment.
They had become so concerned, so absorbed with their own well-
being—their possible future prosperity, blessing and success—
that they lost their sense of community, their sense of corporate
existence. They forgot their God-given mandate to act as one
people, instead becoming very individualistic and self-minded.

From this we might draw some parallels for the Church
today. It seems to me that the Anglo expression of Christ and the
Kingdom—that is, the Church in North America—in viewing its
own prosperity and rightful inheritance, has forgotten its connectedness to the other parts of the Body of Christ. And yet every
American citizen can trace his or her ancestral origins to some
other part of the world; they are all descendants of people who
came here in search of a better life.

When Native believers came to Christ, they were never
embraced and cared for as a legitimate part of the Body of
Christ. They remained outside the Church walls, were not given
safe haven and were encouraged to develop their own churches
away from White churches. Native people have remained a dis-
connected evangelistic field, seen only as a needy people.

Fortunately, the Gadites and Reubenites had a change of
heart. They repented for their self-preserving and self-centered
attitudes. They agreed not to seek their place until all the other
Israelites had first received their rightful inheritance. They
agreed to give up their place temporarily for the sake of their
brethren. Theirs became an all-for-one-and-one-for-all mind-set.

The Lord is calling us all back to an awareness and appreciation of our connectedness in Christ Jesus. Reconciliation is a giant step toward community. Our concern for one another should transcend denominational and doctrinal distinctives, historical traditions and ethnic differences. Unity, cooperation and colaboring in the work of the Kingdom is the call issuing from the throne of grace in our day.

Turtles, rabbits and snails, walking, hurrying and waiting for one another—it's a cool picture.

CHAPTER NINE

WORLD CHRISTIAN GATHERING OF INDIGENOUS PEOPLE

During our lives we sometimes experience events that permanently change our outlook on life. The following is an account of my involvement with the World Christian Gathering of Indigenous People. It brought tsunami-like waves of affirmation from God's heart to my own about the direction we were heading concerning the importance of indigenous culture in our Christian experience. The conference also forever cemented in my own spirit the loving design and purpose God has for the cultural expressions of His people.

WELCOMED AS GUESTS IN THEIR LAND

In November 1996, in a remote part of the world, the sleepy and picturesque town of Rotorua, New Zealand, witnessed a turning point in modern Church history. The inaugural World Christian

Gathering of Indigenous People (WCGIP) signaled the emergence of indigenous people as a critical factor in God's purposes
for the nations. I heard and saw there the advent of a new song
of reconciliation for the Church coming from indigenous people. Centuries of pain resulting from rejection by their colonial
brethren had given birth to a word of forgiveness and healing for
the Body of Christ.

It was a cool, overcast Sunday afternoon on Lake Rotorua, a
beautiful body of water surrounded by lush green hills. I
watched as a war canoe, or *waka*, glided toward us on the water.
As it drew nearer I could hear the man who was standing in the
center singing a rhythmic Maori chant. The shirtless oarsmen
were singing and paddling in cadence to his song.

The waka was a large hollowed-out log with intricate
designs carved along the sides and large carved figures on both
ends—an amazing work of art. Before I stepped into the waka, I
greeted the 20 oarsmen in Lakota. With big, warm smiles they
in turn greeted me in the Maori language. I was a member of
one tribe being honored as a guest by another. There was no
sense of time, only history and wonder, as we moved across the
lake, chanting and rowing.

Prince Mangosuthu Buthelezi (of the Zulu Nation of
South Africa) and I were being ceremonially rowed across part
of Lake Rotorua as representatives of indigenous peoples for
the traditional Maori welcome, or *powhiri*. The powhiri is the
official Maori welcome to "live in the land." We were lifted out
and carried from the waka to the sandy shore by several of the
muscular oarsmen. We walked up the beach, where we joined
several hundred waiting people from various countries, many
colorfully dressed.

Together we proceeded to the ceremonial grounds. Walking
four abreast down the isle of the outdoor courtyard, we stopped

at the edge. Across the tiled court from us was seated a large delegation of Maori elders and dignitaries. Most prominent among them was a powerfully built Maori warrior standing with a spear in his hand. Wearing only a reed skirt and a fierce glare, he began to make his way toward us, dancing rhythmically to a haunting Maori chant. As he skillfully and threateningly brandished a beautifully carved spear, his actions and demeanor were cause for even the bravest to question if this was really a welcome. His dance ended 15 feet in front of us. He then gracefully bent and placed a small leafy twig on the ground. He was issuing a Maori challenge/welcome to us to come as guests in their land. Prince Buthelezi accepted his challenge on our behalf by walking forward and picking up the twig. The air was filled with drama and dignity. In my heart I felt proud and humbled to be a First Nations man.

The solemnity and regality of this powhiri was a prelude, a glimpse of heaven where one day people from every tribe, tongue and nation will gather before the great King. Members of Maori royalty, tribal chiefs and various dignitaries eloquently shared their words of welcome and gratitude, many in their native language. An Australian brother played a traditional Aboriginal welcome on the *digereedoo*, a hollow wind instrument. Elijah Harper of the Cree Nation, a member of the Canadian parliament, presented the queen of the Maori with a beautiful beaded bracelet.

To conclude our time together, the Maori elders formed a line across the courtyard facing us, and we began on one side to shake their hands while they greeted us in the Maori way. Their customary greeting is to press noses together. It is an intimate greeting of exchanging breath, life or spirit with another. Initially uncomfortable, I grew to appreciate the closeness I quickly began to feel with these people.

THEY CAME FROM AROUND THE WORLD

God's handiwork was evident in the beauty and unique grace of the more than 2,000 people from 32 countries and 100 nations who attended this inaugural event hosted by the Maori people of Aoteroa, New Zealand. Because I have lived in Alaska, the beautiful international diversity of this gathering reminded me of the awe and wonder inspired by a spectacular Northern Lights concert of light, color, motion and beauty.

We were deeply touched and

wept openly as different

nations offered their tradition-

al songs and dances of praise

in honor of Jesus Christ.

From around the world came the Saami (reindeer people or Laplanders) from Norway; First Nations from the United States and Canada; Maori of New Zealand; Aborigines from Australia; Zulu from South Africa; and tribes from the countries of Tonga, Fiji, Israel, Hawaii, Irian Jaya, Nagaland (near Nepal), the Solomon Islands, the Cook Islands, China, the Philippines, Samoa, India and many more. Added to this collage of tribal expressions was the whole spectrum of church traditions, including Baptist, Pentecostal, Presbyterian, Anglican and others.

My dear friend and principal organizer, Monte Ohia, a dignified and fatherly Maori elder, said, "While indigenous peoples' conferences have been convened in other parts of the world, this is the first time there has been a worldwide Christian gathering for indigenous peoples." Monte said he was happy that the issues of cultural identity were being discussed openly and hoped this would lead to greater understanding of how culture fits in with traditional Christianity. Of his own experience he said, "When I became a Christian, people were telling me, 'You've got to give up all that Maori stuff now.' I couldn't understand that. I was born a Maori. I was a Maori then and when I die, I'll still be Maori. God is teaching us how to be Christian and indigenous."

SHARING CULTURAL TREASURES

Throughout the eight days of the gathering, people and reports came from many parts of the globe, but the story was always the same. The heartache and loss from colonization, cultural oppression and the loss of identity in the name of Christianization, which you could hear and see and feel in people's emotions, were common threads uniting us as indigenous peoples. I was startled at how universal and common our struggles and experiences have been as native peoples who experienced European colonization. The Motolon of Columbia, the Saami of Norway, the Aborigine of Australia, the Eskimo of the Arctic, the Cherokee of America—their suffering has been the same.

As I listened to the pain and observed the tears of grief and loss of indigenous people from generations of pain and rejection, one thing was evident: There was a glaring absence of bitterness and resentment. Any hearts that still questioned and harbored ill feelings were softened by deep-seated words of forgiveness, reconciliation and healing at the heart of what was said.

On more than one occasion we were deeply touched and wept openly when the Holy Spirit visited us as different nations offered their traditional songs and dances of praise in honor of Jesus Christ. For some of the delegations, even after decades of serving the Lord, this was the first time they had felt free to use their tribal songs and dances for worship. This was especially true of the Native American, Saami and Australian Aboriginal delegations.

Leena, a striking and colorfully dressed young Saami, excitedly shared her newly discovered treasure of dance. She said the past year was the first in the history of the Saami that believers drummed, danced and sang in their traditional style of singing called *yoik* in praise and worship to Jesus Christ. Her pastor remarked how their previous generations had been told that, because of how they were used in the past, the yoik and their dances were evil and could not be used for God. Yet all present at this gathering agreed the Saami presentation was one of the highlights of the gathering, and many openly wept when the Saami sang and danced before the Lord with their "new song."

NEWFOUND FREEDOM FOR
NATIVE AMERICANS

Approximately 30 Native North Americans from the United States and Canada entered the sports center and slowly walked in a clockwise procession in a traditional-style grand entry, some wearing traditional regalia. We were accompanied by a David Ruis worship song entitled "Let the River Flow," sung in part in the Saulteax language. In single file we marched and danced around the interior of the arena until we reached the center aisle in the back. I then called my blond-haired, blue-eyed wife to my side and, hand in hand, we led the delegation to the front as we danced a traditional friendship dance. Many told us later that just the sight of us dancing in a traditional way, as a cross-cultural couple, was living proof that reconciliation is possible in Jesus Christ. As we all stood facing the audience, we could see many were crying and rejoicing before the Lord.

A report reached us the next day that five Maori people, including one who had been in prison, prayed to receive Jesus Christ because they were so deeply touched by our entrance, our music and our dance. One Maori brother said he began weeping when we entered and could not stop for the next hour because of the presence of God and the beauty of the Lord he saw in us. Later, an Aboriginal man from Australia shared his joy with us: When he saw us dancing, he had joined us and danced in the traditional style of his own tribe. He said it was the first time he had felt the liberty to do so as a Christian. He was released, blessed and affirmed by the Lord as he danced.

The day after our presentation, a brother from the Coastal Salish Reserve in British Columbia told me that before he came to the gathering he was opposed to using the traditional-style songs and dances in worship to Jesus Christ. After experiencing the presence of the Holy Spirit, the beauty of the Lord and how deeply impacted the people were, he said he had changed his position 180 degrees. He now planned to seek the Lord to find ways to redeem what the devil had stolen from his people and to see their traditional cultural expressions sanctified for God's glory and the Church's use.

NOT TOURIST ATTRACTIONS OR HOLLYWOOD CHARACTERS

During the indigenous conference, Reverend Little, a pastor from the Philippines, gave a brief history of missions among the tribes in his country:

Among our people, to be Christian had come to mean to be westernized. Most mainstream Filipinos became alienated from their own indigenous culture. It was labeled pagan, demonic and equated with witchcraft and paganism. . . . As Christians finally realized they could be Christian and indigenous, they were overjoyed. A ministry has formed to rediscover our dances, music and native arts as gifts from God. We must take the stigma off of indigenous culture, and sing and dance to the Lord. This is our patrimony as God's children.[1]

Pastor Little's speech expressed the sentiments of what God was doing during the gathering:

It is a wellspring of joy to see our brothers and sisters dancing—not as anthropological curiosities, not as tourist attractions, not as Hollywood specialties—but as God's children. As long as song and dance are only for tourists, we have not won. The Church must be the sanctuary of the arts of song and dance, not the cemetery. The Church is the patron of the arts and should be for Native people as well. We need to move forward into the twenty-first century as who we are.[2]

One of the goals of the organizers was to affirm the God-given cultural gifts of tribal people. Monte Ohia said:

In the Church there is a continuum. On the one hand there are those who think nothing Native should be allowed in Christianity, and on the opposite pole, those who don't want anything if it isn't Native as well as Christian. Somewhere in between lies wisdom. This is what we need to pray for, that the Lord may recover what He wants to cherish and redeem from all the varieties of culture, songs and dances He has so delightfully created.[3]

On Tuesday afternoon, as the auditorium lights were dimmed, one spotlight lit up a rough wooden cross on the stage. Without a word, two Australian Aboriginal men gracefully danced in and reverently laid their Aboriginal instruments, cultural forms and dance, as well as the Word of God, at the foot of the cross. Then they received them back as gifts from the Creator, only now to be used for His glory and honor. This beautiful depiction of Jesus' redemptive power painted a magnificent picture for us of God's ultimate power to save and make new the people and cultures of this world for His glory. A brother said that what he saw in the redemption of the Aboriginal digereedoo was a picture of God breathing healing into the land of Australia.

The gathering ended on Sunday afternoon with a challenge for all indigenous nations to pursue God and His will for us, to be bridge builders within our nations and between our nations. Despite the injustices of the past and present, we must choose the higher road of love and forgiveness if our people are to be free and healthy again. After all I saw and experienced, as the Body of Christ we have much to anticipate and to receive from our indigenous brothers and sisters around the world and down the street.

A White brother spoke of being acutely aware of the fact that the treasure of indigenous people generally continues to be excluded from the Church and that, as a result, the Church rarely has the benefit of "drinking from their wells." The gathering made me realize more than ever before that this is a story the Church around the earth needs to hear and see.

The second WCGIP was hosted by the First Nations of North America in Rapid City, South Dakota, in August 1998; and the third by the Aborigines in Sydney, Australia, in January 2000. There is a great stirring that continues to grow worldwide, even as stories of rejoicing and hope continue to be told and new freedoms in Christ are discovered.

CHAPTER TEN

NATIVE AMERICANS AND WORLD MISSIONS

The warm, pleasant night air of Wellington, New Zealand's capital city, felt great as the streets were alive with thousands of people talking, walking and enjoying the late-night street life. As my hosts and I were walking about, we came upon a group of street performers. Walking around several people who were juggling pins and twirling flaming spears, I approached the apparent leader of the street musicians. I introduced myself as a Lakota/Sioux Indian from America and asked him if I could borrow one of their drums and sing a traditional Lakota song when they took a break. He immediately replied, "Far out!" and said they would be honored. As a matter of fact, he said the reason they were there was to perform a dedication ceremony for the grand opening of a new pub. He then asked me if I would like to come upstairs to the establishment and sing my songs along with theirs. I immediately replied, "Far out!" and said I would love to.

In the pub the air was heavy with cigarette and marijuana smoke, as well as the sounds of people talking and laughing. After the musicians finished playing a few songs, the leader grabbed me by the arm and took me up on the main stage. He introduced me as a Sioux Indian who had come all the way from America and then told them I was going to play a traditional drum song.

I had been praying that the Spirit of God would take my words and transcend the barriers of language to speak to their hearts and spirits. I talked to them of the first man and first woman's departure from the Creator's path of beauty, how they had chosen a different path that had caused them to become lost and wander in darkness. I told them how their lostness had broken the heart of the Creator and that He knew they could never find their way back to the path of beauty. So He chose to come to the earth and live among them and show them how to get back on that path. I then sang, in the Lakota language, a traditional-style worship song I had written:

> I am walking with God my Creator
> I am walking with the One who saves me—Jesus Christ
> I am walking on this road

I then said a few words about the audience's journey and challenged them, asking whether or not they were living their lives on the Creator's path of beauty. They applauded and I walked off the stage. My Native culture had opened the door in a dark place and, for a brief moment, enabled me to bring some light into the lives of people who would never look for help from the Church.

NATIVES AROUND THE WORLD

My experience in New Zealand was not a one-time occurrence. God is using Native people around the world to bring the gospel to various cultures.

Natives in Mongolia

On my 1993 trip to Ulaanbaater, the capital city of Mongolia, I stopped in Japan and also spent a few days in Beijing, China. Everywhere we walked, especially in China, people gawked. They had never seen "Red Indians from America" before.

In Mongolia, however, the people immediately identified with us as a tribal people. In fact, as we traveled to some remote areas, we were informed that many Mongol people believe we are their relatives. They spoke of legends about a group of Mongol hunters who traveled to the north and the east and never returned; they believed we were descendents of those hunters, their distant cousins. This being the case, the people felt curious, but also safe, and they trusted us. Simply because we were Native Americans, we had the attention of these Mongol listeners and were able to freely share the gospel story.

Natives in Israel

At the beginning of this book, I told the story of my trip with my friend Garland to Jerusalem. While we were there, several other instances occurred that confirmed in my own heart the love and interest other people have for the First Nations people.

One afternoon Garland and I went to the Wailing Wall to pray and to intercede for our Native people. A reporter from the Jerusalem Post stopped us and asked if he could take our picture. He told us the Israelis had never before seen Native American people praying at the Wailing Wall. This was evident as many people stared and made comments about our presence.

Garland and I were part of the International Intercessory Prayer Conference in Jerusalem, which was attended by people from 146 nations. During one of the evening sessions, Garland and I, along with another friend named Joe Venezia, were to give a report of God's work among the tribes of North America. I came out dressed in my beaded buckskin war shirt and headpiece, feathers and all. There were cheers, applause and rejoicing to see the Red Indians from America. I shared my vision to take teams of Native performers—singers and dancers—overseas to communicate the gospel through our Indian cultures. Afterward, one man said he didn't know there were any Indians who were Christians. People from about a dozen different countries came to me and said they believed that if we brought a Native team to their countries, we would draw tens of thousands of people who would come to see the Red Indians.

In 1999, more than 80 First Nations believers participated in the Feast of Tabernacles in Jerusalem. The delegation led the international worship procession through the city and was invited to present a traditional drum honor song in the Israeli Knesset—a very great honor. Afterward, the delegation was invited to meet in the private chambers of the Speaker of the Knesset, Avram Bourg, the second most powerful political leader in Israel. Lynda Prince and other tribal leaders presented him with a drum, beaded moccasins, a full feather headdress and other gifts. He in turn pledged the full protection and blessing of Israel for the team during their time in Israel.

Natives in Hollywood

As detrimental as Hollywood's negative stereotypical portrayal of Native people has been, it nonetheless has given worldwide exposure to Indian culture. We have long been portrayed as having big noses and a two-word vocabulary—*ugh* and *how!* And despite a mysterious, almost superhuman tie to the land—supposedly we could tell how many geese were flying overhead by the breeze, and we knew when a deer was born in the forest presumably because of a disturbance in "the Force"—we always lost the wars, even if we outnumbered the cowboys 75 to 1!

In recent years movies like *Dances with Wolves, Thunderheart, 500 Nations, Last of the Mohicans* and *Geronimo* have portrayed Native people in a much more accurate light. The incredible reception and accolades given to *Dances with Wolves* has revealed a sense of guilt and fascination with Native culture in America, even worldwide. I was told in Holland that there it is the most widely watched movie ever.

In large part because of the movies, we are perhaps the best-known people group on the face of the earth today. God can even use Hollywood for His redemptive purposes!

Natives in New Zealand

At the inaugural World Christian Gathering of Indigenous People in November of 1996, I asked several hundred Maori men if they had ever, as little boys, played cowboys and Indians. Much to my surprise, almost to the man, they enthusiastically raised their hands and voiced that they had. So I asked how many wanted to be the cowboys. None raised their hands. I asked how many wanted to be the Indians, and they all raised their hands! A few even shouted war cries. How is it that these Maori warriors, literally on the other side of the world in New Zealand, would so strongly identify with Indians from America's old West? It is interesting to note, however, that unlike the Maori, my boyhood friends on the reservation all wanted to be the cowboys because in the movies the Indians always lost.

Natives in Fiji

One morning I was enjoying a talk with a couple of the local hotel staff in Fiji. We shared some tribal customs and beliefs and our common faith in Jesus Christ. A wrinkled old man told me how he hated the way American Indians had been treated in our own country. He encouraged me to remain strong and to be proud of who God made me as an Indian.

While in Fiji, I asked a younger man in his late 20s if he had ever played cowboys and Indians as a boy. He laughed and said he had. He said they used to cut their shorts and the sleeves of their shirts and pockets into strips to resemble leather fringe, and they made bows and arrows and chased each other around.

Native Spirituality and the New Age

The New Age movement has really latched on to Native spirituality. In any New Age store today you will find all types of Native articles of clothing, herbs and items used for traditional ceremonies. There are music tapes, pipes, ceremonial objects and even Indian tarot cards—much to the chagrin and displeasure of Christian and non-Christian Native spiritual leaders.

While in New Zealand I went into a small record store at a local mall, and right on the front counter was a rack of North American Native trinkets—all genuine Indian-made stuff from Thailand! You could buy a tiny buffalo with a piece of turquoise and a special prayer for strength from the buffalo. I couldn't believe it! In any New Age store around the world you will find our First Nations cultural artifacts being used to promote a false faith.

On the other hand, I understand that my Native culture can be a powerful inroad into the New Age community, which is often antagonistic and vehemently opposed to Christianity. This gives me as a Native man a unique opportunity to present Jesus Christ as the Son of the Creator, come to earth with power and spiritual wisdom and healing for the people.

Natives in the Former Communist Bloc

During the Cold War era of American and Soviet relations, the Soviets used the plight of Indian people in their anti-America propaganda. Whenever the United States decried human rights violations in the Soviet Union's treatment of political and social dissidents, the Soviets would cite the inhumanity of American treatment of Native people, questioning the right of the Americans to accuse them of anything worse. The Soviets told people throughout the Communist bloc that the United States had imprisoned her Native American citizens in concentration camps called reservations. They further portrayed Native people as the downtrodden folk heroes of the American capitalistic system.

A number of years ago, when I was pastoring, a Hungarian couple named Mihaly and Emese Sczanto began attending our church shortly after they fled to the United States from Budapest, Hungary. They told me that the Hungarians loved Native culture and said their people would come by the tens of thousands to attend a cultural event featuring Indians from America. They felt people would easily fill soccer stadiums and auditoriums for such an event.

As a result of Cold War propaganda, there is in Russia and the surrounding nations a great deal of empathy for and deep interest in American Indians. I have been told by several others who also immigrated from former Soviet bloc countries that if we were to bring a team of Indians to stage an Indian cultural performance, we would fill the largest stadiums and auditoriums in any city there.

Natives in China

As the curtain opened, the silhouette of two men took shape through the blue fog shrouding the stage. The rhythm of their drum could be heard throughout the auditorium where more than a thousand Chinese people waited for the "Red Indians." From each side of the stage came a dancer as the audience applauded and cheered. First, from the right emerged an older male traditional dancer; then, from the left, another traditional dancer; then, alternately, a grass dancer, a fancy dancer, a female traditional dancer and two female fancy shawl dancers.

In May of 1999, in the humid climate of Yunan, a southern province in the People's Republic of China, 11 of us First Nations artists and dancers shared our cultural talents. The Native Warriors team was part of an outreach sponsored by the International Festival of the Arts, which invited us to share our God-given talents with the Chinese people.

Art Begay, a Lakota/Navajo, and I were asked to assemble a Christian Native cultural team. We invited several Native believers to be part of a team that performed in a variety of venues in the city of Kunming. Various members shared their traditional dances, drum songs, painting, pottery and music. Art said that, though his Warriors for Christ ministry team has been to Hawaii and Germany, he was humbled and made to feel unworthy by the incredibly positive response the team received from the Chinese people.

Jonathon Maracle is founder and leader of Broken Walls, a Canadian music group from Tyendinaga Mohawk Territory. He and Kris DeLorenzi sang contemporary and traditional Mohawk chants to very appreciative Chinese listeners. Many of the students especially enjoyed Jonathon's beautiful and lifelike bird whistles and flute playing on the Loon Song. A young Chinese woman who served as an interpreter wrote in her best

English to Jonathon, "Your great music give me a deep impression and your Indian story. I really appreciate what you have done."

Another Chinese interpreter said to Dan LaPlante, a Lakota grass dancer, "Other performers good . . . but Indians, you are the best." This was a significant compliment in light of the fact that more than 200 professional artists and performers from 20 different countries participated in the festival.

An immediate bond formed between the Chinese people and the First Nations delegation—a bond that transcended time, history, distance, culture and language. Because Yunan Province has the highest percentage of indigenous tribal groups in China, there were many connections with the people as fellow tribal members. This was highlighted on one occasion when our team performed at a major arts university. We would share a dance; then students from one of the local tribes would share a dance. This exchange of songs and dances went on for more than two hours and concluded with everyone dancing and laughing together and with our giving gifts to the senior faculty members.

Elmer Yazzie, a Navajo traditional Yucca brush painter, commented, "There was a spirit of trust between us; a kindred spirit was obvious." He said, "I was deeply touched by the Chinese. Several times I cried for us—our people and their people."[1]

One of the singing groups in the festival was the well-known American quartet A Cappella. One of their singers, Gary Moyers, made this observation about the First Nations team:

The Chinese seemed overwhelmed by the Native cultural expressions. First Nations people have, over the years, attained a level of respect and "mystique" that is very attractive to others. . . . To have these cultural expressions equated with Jesus Christ is very powerful![2]

Fern Cloud-Chief Eagle, a Dakota traditional and hoop dancer, drew great applause and appreciation from audiences. Her hoop dancing was a huge favorite with the people. Fern said about her dancing, "When I dance, I do it as unto the Lord. I never think of dancing as performing. It's more like worship and celebration to me." She was impacted significantly by her time in China. She said of her experience, "I was made aware of how short I fall from being what God intends for me. It has been a tremendous realization of responsibility and spiritual growth in Christ."[3]

As team members, we were all very honored to have Dr. Jerry Yellowhawk, a Lakota traditional dancer, as the elder for the team. Several of the Chinese commented on what a wise and calm man he was. After witnessing the response the team received, Dr. Yellowhawk said, "I believe that our redeemed cultures can be used in world missions. I am deeply moved with compassion. We must endeavor to reach our world with the good news at any cost." He also said, "I was surprised that the Chinese peoples responded to our Native traditional songs and dancing in such a positive way."[4]

One afternoon several of us were invited to make a special presentation at a deaf and blind school. Both the deaf and blind were able to receive something they enjoyed immensely. At the conclusion of our time with the students and staff, I led many of the smiling students and faculty in a friendship dance around the multipurpose area, and soon all of us were laughing, clapping and cheering one another. Again we were led by the Lord to honor the faculty for their work, and we gave them gifts.

At an early-morning assembly we witnessed 1,500 brightly dressed 6- to 12-year-old children march with great precision and in exact formation into the school courtyard for a program with our team. Their entrance and corporate morning-exercise regimen was a program to behold. At one point, fancy dancer Art

Begay danced down an aisle, with feathers, ribbons and fringe flying, out into the young crowd. The children were mesmerized by him and got so excited that many of them formed little serpentine lines and danced with him around the courtyard. We were then pleasantly surprised as a group of 10 of the children sang a song in English especially prepared for us: "Ten Little Indians." At the finish each team member was given a gift by the students.

God, through our experience in China, had confirmed to each of us in a very clear and undeniable way that He has indeed prepared the way for First Nations believers to go into all the world as ambassadors of the gospel. Already some of our team members have received invitations to Cameroon, Nigeria, Ethiopia, South Africa, Israel, Switzerland, Germany, England, the Czech Republic, Australia, New Zealand and Indonesia.

God has prepared the way for the First Nations to go into all the world as ambassadors of the gospel.

One of the highlights of the trip was to see how a group of First Nations believers with a common vision could work effectively as a team, even though we were from diverse backgrounds. We represented Wesleyan, Baptist, Nazarene, charismatic and Pentecostal traditions. Various tribal backgrounds were also represented, including Mohawk, Lakota, Cherokee, Dakota, Wyendot and Navajo. Reaching lost people with the good news was the vision and purpose that drew us together, rather than lifting up culture, denomination or religious traditions.

Jesus Christ is the Waymaker, and He unmistakably made a way for our team into the hearts of the Chinese people. It was obvious from the Chinese people's overwhelming response that God will use the traditional cultural expressions of dance, drumming, singing, language, regalia and the fine arts of First Nations people for His honor and glory.

I believe the question facing the Church today is whether or not the Body of Christ will recognize this divine opportunity and be willing to partner with and follow the lead of their First Nations brethren. Another question is whether or not First Nations believers will take advantage of this global opportunity to go into all the world and make a difference in the lives of unbelievers by communicating the good news through the bridge of their God-given cultural expressions.

BORN FOR SUCH A TIME AS THIS

I see that, through the vehicle of our culture and by God's providence, we as Native Americans can visit any country of the world and be immediately welcomed and trusted. Because of our culture and unique history, made known around the world through books and movies, more than any other people group we can travel anywhere and be received as ambassadors for the Kingdom. We need to take advantage of this as God's providence. I believe this is part of God's plan for restoring Native people to their God-given place in the Body of Christ.

One person has said that perhaps Native people are being raised up as a last-days generation of world-class evangelists for this final hour. My response: Why not? I believe that in the history of modern missions, no other people group is so uniquely positioned for world evangelization as First Nations people are today!

Who are these Native leaders God is raising up in this generation? What will it take to see the release of Native ministers throughout the world? What kinds of partnerships must be formed to make this dream come to life?

For centuries, Native people have been on the receiving end of missionary endeavors. The time has come for us to move from being the recipients of missions to that of being *participants* in missions. "I long for the day when, from Native churches, we will be sending out qualified, Spirit-filled Native missionaries to the uttermost parts of the earth!"[5]

YOU CAN MAKE A DIFFERENCE

As Native people emerge to take their place alongside their Caucasian, African-American, Hispanic and Asian brethren in the Body of Christ, we will all be better for it. My prayer is that after having read this book you will embrace God's heart for Native people. I hope you will become a proactive advocate for Native believers, both in prayer and in relationships. I hope you will find a way to partner with Native ministry leaders and organizations.

If we, as Native followers of Jesus, are to emerge from our pain and absence to find our place in the Body of Christ, we need the love and help of all our brethren. Can we be seen as equal partners by the rest of the Body of Christ? Will we be allowed to develop new ways of doing church that honor God's purposes for the creative expression of our cultures? Will new ministry partnerships and coalitions form? Will you help be a part of this wonderful process of reconciliation, restoration and release?

HOHECETUWE LO! — "THAT'S THE WAY IT IS!"

FIRST NATIONS MINISTRY PARTNERS

Dr. Jerry Yellowhawk (Lakota/Sioux Nation)
District Superintendent
Wesleyan Native American Ministries
P.O. Box 7038
Rapid City, SD 57709

Pastor Steve Cheremie (Chittimacha, Choctaw Nations)
Word of Life Church
P.O. Box 141
Gretna, LA 70054-0141

Mary Glazier (Haida Nation)
President
Windwalkers International
4731 Mars Drive
Anchorage, AK 99507

Rev. Adrian Jacobs
(Cayuga, Six Nations Iroquois Confederacy)
Outreach Worker
Lutheran Assoc. of Missionaries and Pilots (LAMP-US)
612 Wood Avenue
Rapid City, SD 57701

Ray Aldred (Cree Nation)
National Director
First Nations Alliance Churches of Canada
746 Hayworth Crescent
Regina, SK, S4X 1Y1 Canada

Jon Lansa (Hopi)
Native American Director
Mentoring/Coaching Native Leaders
Navigators
lansaj@msn.com

Pastor Dean Shingoose (Saulteaux Nation)
Calgary Native Pentecostal Church
257 Laguna Circle N.E.
Calgary, AB, T1Y 6W4 Canada

Doug Yates (Haida, Tsimsian Nations)
Founder
Young Warriors
10290 Arborvitae Drive
Anchorage, AK 99507

Jonathan Maracle (Mohawk Nation)
Broken Walls
RR1 234 Bayshore Road
Tyendinaga Territory, ON, K0K 1X0 Canada

Rev. Terry LeBlanc (Mi'kmaq Nation, Acadian)
Manager, Aboriginal Programs
World Vision Canada
P.O. Box 295
Evansburg, AB T0E 070

Fern Noble (Cree Nation)
International Reconciliation Coalition
606 Princess Drive
Oxnard, CA 93030

Rita Bear-Gray (Cree Nation)
Intercessor and artisan
5204 S. 354th Street
Auburn, WA 98001

Dr. Suuqiina (Inuit Nation)
Inuit Ministries International
P.O. Box 339
Portland, TN 37148

Randy Woodley (Keetoowah Cherokee)
Eagle's Wings Ministries
1705 Joy Road
Hayden, AL 35079

Kyle Taylor (Pawnee)
Pastor, Liberty Faith Center
Cofounder, White Eagle Ministry
P.O. Box 931
Glenpool, OK 74033

Introduction

1. Tom Claus and Dale Kietzman, *Christian Leadership in Indian America* (Chicago: Moody Press, 1976), p. 8.

Chapter 1

1. Dr. R. Pierce Beaver, *The Native American Christian Community: A Directory of Indian, Aleut and Eskimo Churches* (Monrovia, CA: MARC, 1979), pp. 31, 46.
2. Dr. Paul Hiebert, *Anthropological Reflections on Missiological Issues* (Grand Rapids, MI: Baker Books, 1994), pp. 54, 55.
3. L. Frank Baum, *Aberdeen (SD) Saturday Pioneer*, December 20, 1890, quoted in *Native Wind* 2, no. 1 (1997).
4. George Russell, *American Indian Facts of Life* (Phoenix, AZ: Russell Publications, 1997), n.p.
5. Ibid.
6. David A. Rausch and Blair Schlepp, *Native American Voices* (Grand Rapids, MI: Baker Books, 1994), p. 61.
7. Ibid.
8. Ibid, p. 59.
9. Ibid.
10. Ibid.
11. Russell, *American Indian Facts of Life*, n.p.
12. Robert A. Ryan, "Native American Indian Cultural Risk Factors—Contact to Termination" (lecture handout, October 1996).
13. David Wallace Adams, *Education for Extinction: American Indians and the Boarding School Experience 1875-1928* (Lawrence, KS: University of Kansas Press, 1995), p. 51.
14. Ryan, "Native American Indian Cultural Risk Factors."
15. Adams, *Education for Extinction*.
16. David Tavernier, e-mail sent from Lighthouse Full Gospel Center, Parrish, Florida (October 1993).
17. Russell, *American Indian Facts of Life*, pp. 9, 57.

Chapter 2

1. Michael S. Horton, *Beyond Culture Wars* (Chicago: Moody Press, 1994), p. 177.
2. Francis Paul Prucha, *Documents of United States Indian Policy* (Lincoln, NE: University of Nebraska, 1990), p. 77.
3. Lloyd Martin, *One Faith, Two Peoples: Communicating Across Cultures Within the Church* (Paraparaumu, New Zealand: Salt Company, 1991), pp. 25, 26.

Chapter 3

1. Horton, *Beyond Culture Wars*, pp. 169, 176, 177.
2. Dr. Charles Kraft, *Anthropology for Christian Witness* (Maryknoll, NY: Orbis Books, 1996), n.p.
3. Sosene Le'au, *Called to Honor Him: How Men and Women Are Redeeming Cultures* (Tampa, FL: CultureCom Press, 1997), p. 138.
4. Source unknown.
5. Chief William Red Fox, *Memoirs of Chief Red Fox* (New York: McGraw-Hill, 1971), pp. 15-18.

Chapter 4

1. Peter Nabakov, *Native American Testimony* (New York: Penguin Books, 1991), p. 57.
2. John Fisher, *What on Earth Are We Doing?—Finding Our Place as Christians in the World* (Ann Arbor, MI: Servant Publications, 1996), p. 19.
3. Ibid., pp. 20, 29, 30.
4. Source unknown.

Chapter 5

1. Lowell Hurst, *Satan's Music Exposed* (Rossville, GA: Grapevine Books, 1980), p. 105.
2. Harold M. Best, *Music Through the Eyes of Faith* (San Francisco: Harper and Row, 1993), pp. 54, 72.
3. Rev. Adrian Jacobs, "Syncretism: The Meeting of the Two Roads."
4. Rose, "Steal My Rage," ed. Joel T. Maki, *New Native Voices* (Vancouver, BC: Douglas and McIntyre, 1995), p. 37.

Chapter 6

1. Zeb Bradford Long and Douglas McMurry, *The Collapse of the Brass Heaven: Rebuilding Our Worldview to Embrace the Power of God* (Grand Rapids, MI: Chosen Books), pp. 209-216.
2. Thomas E. Jessett, *Chief Spokane Garry: Christian, Statesman and Friend of the Whiteman* (Minneapolis, MN: T.S. Denison, 1960), p. 22.
3. Ibid., p. 24.
4. Ibid., p. 35.
5. Ibid.
6. Clifford Merrill Drury, *The Diaries and Letters of Henry Harmon Spalding and Asa Bowen Smith Relating to Nez Perce Mission* (Glendale, CA: Arthur H. Clark, 1958), p. 78.
7. Ibid., p. 35.
8. Ibid., pp. 78, 79.
9. Ibid., p. 78.

10. Ibid., p. 47.
11. William S. Lewis, *The Case of Spokane Garry* (Fairfield, WA: Ye Galleon Press, 1987), p. 57.
12. Jessett, *Chief Spokane Garry: Christian, Statesman and Friend of the Whiteman*, p. 173.
13. Ibid.
14. Ibid., p. 208.
15. Ibid.
16. E. T. Becher, "Chief Spokane Garry's Bibles and Descendents," *Spokane (WA) Spokesman-Review*, May 24, 1953.
17. Ibid.

Chapter 7
1. John Dawson, *Healing America's Wounds* (Ventura, CA: Regal Books, 1996), p. 30.
2. *Little Big Man*, Cinema Center 100 Productions/Stockbridge-Hiller Productions/20th Century Fox Film Corporation, Los Angeles, 1970.

Chapter 9
1. Reverend Little, speech presented at World Christian Gathering of Indigenous People (Rotorua, New Zealand, November 1996).
2. Ibid.
3. Monte Ohia, speech presented at World Christian Gathering of Indigenous People (Rotorua, New Zealand, November 1996).

Chapter 10
1. Elmer Yazzie, response to personal questionnaire from the author, May 1999.
2. Gary Moyers, response to personal questionnaire from the author, May 1999.
3. Fern Cloud-Chief Eagle, response to personal questionnaire from the author, May 1999.
4. Dr. Jerry Yellowhawk, response to personal questionnaire from the author, May 1999.
5. Craig Stephen Smith, *Whiteman's Gospel* (Winnipeg, MB: Indian Life Books, 1997), pp. 59, 60.

Wiconi *(wee-choe'-nee)* is a Lakota/Sioux word meaning "life." For more information about Wiconi International or to contact Richard Twiss, please write or call:

Wiconi International
P.O. Box 5246
Vancouver, WA 98668
Phone: (360) 546-1867
Fax: (360) 546-3801
E-mail: wanbli@aol.com
www.wiconi.com

Other Resources Available Through Wiconi...

Culture, Christ, and The Kingdom Study Guide

Presenting Biblical Principles For Native Ministry That Honor God, His People & His Creation
by Richard Twiss

This 69 page study guide establishes a clear Biblical foundation for cross-cultural ministry among First Nations people. It views the cultural expressions of Native people from a positive, affirming, and redemptive point of view, not a rejectionist one. The study guide looks at issues of redefining the use of Native drums, dance, symbols, and regalia (costumes) in a Christian worship context in light of redemption and missiology. It is an excellent introductory level resource that sheds new light on Native cultural viewpoints and expressions that have long been erroneously condemned by the Church. It will equip you to better understand the growing tension in North American missions between true Biblical contextualization and syncretism.

Dancing Our Prayers

Perspectives on Syncretism, Critical Contextualization and Cultural Practices in First Nations Ministry
by Richard Twiss

God the father coming to the earth in the form of a human being is the greatest example of contextualized ministry that ever was. Jesus, who is God, became immersed in the historical, social, religious, linguistic and cultural contexts of the Hebrew people. He became one of us "two-leggeds" in order to communicate cross-culturally to us the truths of the Kingdom of heaven. George Barna has written that the church of America is suffering from the crisis of irrelevance. Nowhere else is this more evident than in Native ministry. However, in the midst of this disturbing report, a "Movement of the Gospel" is emerging in First Nations communities across North America. This booklet presents Biblical perspectives on the issues of syncretism, contextualization, and culture and shows how they impact the fulfillment of the Great Commission of Jesus among Aboriginal Peoples. Behind these perspectives is the burden to discover more effective ways to bring people into a saving relationship with Christ, raise up mature disciples and leaders, and support indigenous church planting efforts across North America. Dancing Our Prayers directs us to the Word of God as our foundation for effective mission and discipleship.

Beautiful Great One
by Jonathan Maracle

Jonathan's latest release of Creator inspired songs will both grip and stir the warrior heart of each listener, as well as lead those whose spirits are restless to where "the waters are still."

The exclamation of my praise arises to a great God who opened the gates of Hell and rescued my brother from drugs, death and rock and roll.

This collection of culturally sensitive and Christ-honoring songs proclaim to the world that the kingdom of darkness will succumb to the advancing kingdom of His dear Son! "And they sent out singers before the army to Praise the Lord." (II Chronicles 20:21). Even so come Lord Jesus! Come in worship, come in music, come in power, come to establish your kingdom in our hearts! "Blessed is the people that know the joyful sound!" (Psalm 89:15).

> Ross Maracle (Brother of Jonathan)
> Director/Host of Spirit Alive TV
> Pastor of The Gathering Place, Toronto

Wiconi Promotional Video

This video gives an overview of our "Dancing Our Prayers" cultural teams that travel internationally to bring the Good News of Jesus Christ through their cultural expressions of drumming and dancing. The teams include pastors, evangelists, musicians and dancers who are committed to presenting the Gospel to Indigenous Peoples in North and South America and around the world. Approximately five minutes long.

1996 Inaugural World Christian Gathering Of Indigenous People
Auckland, New Zealand

In 1996 more than 2000 people from 32 countries met together as guests of the Maori people of New Zealand to celebrate their freedom in Christ as Indigenous believers. It was a beautiful demonstration of how the unique indigenous cultural expressions of traditional dances, instruments, music, and languages of tribal people can be used to worship Jesus Christ. This professional video has been shown to people across North America and many parts of the world, always making a deep spiritual impact on the audience. You will be blessed and encouraged as you watch how the cultural expressions of indigenous people are emerging as legitimate Biblical expressions of Christian faith that truly honors God and edifies the Church. **Video** (20 minutes)

In addition, the Wiconi Resource Center has available for purchase an extensive audio and video tape library addressing a wide range of topics related to First Nations ministry; an assortment of music CDs; and a growing list of books and other written materials. To order a copy of the products highlighted or a resource list, please call our office at 360-546-1867, email at office@wiconi.com, shop online at www.wiconi.com or mail us at P.O. Box 5246, Vancouver, WA 98668.

Richard Twiss, President
WICONI INTERNATIONAL
P.O. Box 5246 Vancouver, WA 98668
360-546-1867 www.wiconi.com

Best-Sellers from Regal

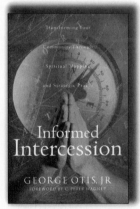
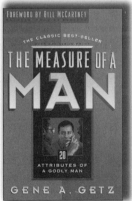
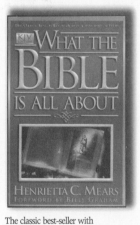

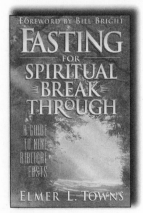
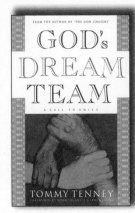
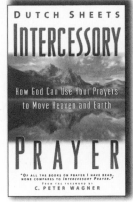

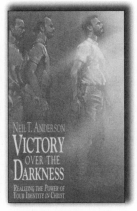
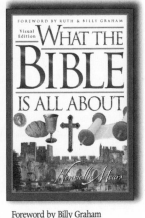